UNIVERSITY OF CHICAGO STUDIES IN LIBRARY SCIENCE

THE FUNCTION OF THE LIBRARY
in the
MODERN COLLEGE

THE FUNCTION OF THE LIBRARY
in the
MODERN COLLEGE

The Nineteenth Annual Conference
of the Graduate Library School
June 14–18, 1954

Edited by HERMAN H. FUSSLER

THE UNIVERSITY OF CHICAGO PRESS
CHICAGO & LONDON

THE UNIVERSITY OF CHICAGO STUDIES IN LIBRARY SCIENCE

The papers in this volume were published originally in the
LIBRARY QUARTERLY, *October 1954*

International Standard Book Number: 0–226–27555–8
Library of Congress Catalog Card Number: 67–28464

THE UNIVERITY OF CHICAGO PRESS, CHICAGO 60637
The University of Chicago Press, Ltd., London

INTRODUCTION

HERMAN H. FUSSLER

THE nineteenth annual conference of the Graduate Library School was directed toward a reappraisal of the place and function of the college library in the four-year college. The objectives, content, and methodology of undergraduate instruction have been the subject of very close scrutiny and general controversy and discussion since the late 1920's and early 1930's. There were, of course, searching appraisals and profound changes in collegiate education prior to this period; yet it seems possible to date the appearance of the current rather general concern with these problems from about this period. While there is still anything but unanimity on the nature of the four-year college curriculum, several rather clear patterns have emerged and now are fairly commonly known. Since most educational authorities, regardless of the particular course of action urged, have tended to assert that the library—if the library was recognized at all—was important to the college program, it seemed reasonable to assume that changes relating to such basic questions as the objectives, content, and methodology of the college might also lead to important changes in the college library. The effects, if any, of these basic curricular changes upon the college library have not been too well defined in the professional literature.

In order to provide for a reasonably systematic approach to this topic, the conference program was divided into three major parts. The first part was directed toward an effort to ascertain the major current educational objectives and their actual relationships to the library. This topic is developed in four papers: "Trends and Developments in Undergraduate Education," "The Relationship between the Library and Collegiate Objectives," "Government and Control of the College Library," and "The Liberal Arts Function of the University Library."

The second part of the conference was given over to an analysis of the major resources that the college library must have to meet its obligations: "The Nature of the Book Collection," "The College-Library Building," "College-Library Personnel," and "The Place of Newer Media in the Undergraduate Program." The concluding sessions of the conference were centered on a general consideration of the financial problems of the college library and an effort to draw together some of the major questions and problems mentioned by the various speakers. That "service" does not appear as a separate topic may appear to be an omission, but, in fact, it seemed impossible to present most of the conference papers without incorporating, both explicitly and implicitly, views and comments upon the extent and character of college-library service. To discuss the nature of book collections without reference to college-library service would, on the face of it, appear to be impossible and ridiculous. Therefore, the many problems of college-library service are treated integrally with the other topics from which they cannot logically be separated.

The papers of the conference do not constitute a definitive description of the function of the library in the modern college—it was not anticipated that they would. They do, however, suggest some of the changes in function that have already occurred and that may be expected to occur in the future in the college library. The papers also describe the considerable variety of problems that these functional changes have produced or are likely to produce. Finally, they strongly confirm the view that the college library is vital to American higher education, that it is well aware of its responsibilities, that, for the most part, it seems to be meeting its obligations successfully, and that further definition and clarification of function is likely to be desirable for some time to come.

TABLE OF CONTENTS

TRENDS AND DEVELOPMENTS IN HIGHER EDUCATION

CARTER DAVIDSON

THE small liberal arts college dominated the scene of American higher education for the first two centuries, from the founding of Harvard in 1636 until the Civil War. In the 1840's there was a grand total of 12,000 students in a hundred small colleges, none of them with more than 500 students. For twenty years before the Civil War the percentage of young men of college age who were actually attending college declined noticeably, and the war itself wrote "finis" to the story of many an institution. The war ended, the nation realized it had come of age and looked about for new forms to embody its new aspirations. Great Britain had lost favor because of her partisanship during the conflict, and the new European power, Germany, conqueror of Austria and led by the impressive Bismarck, was beginning to dominate the scene; as a result, it was to the German universities of Berlin, Munich, Leipzig, Bonn, Freiburg, Heidelberg, Marburg, Jena, Göttingen, or Erlangen rather than to the British Oxford or Cambridge that America turned for her models. In the German universities the stress was upon research, scholarship, and professional preparation for law or medicine or theology rather than upon the old liberal arts. As a result, America turned to the university pattern for her new higher education.

In 1868 Cornell University, under Andrew D. White and partly financed by the federal government through the Land-Grant College Act of Senator Morrill, opened with colleges of engineering, agriculture, and mechanic arts. In 1869 Charles W. Eliot became president of Harvard, and during his forty-year term gave this oldest college its present university structure. In 1875 Vanderbilt University opened its doors in Nashville, with schools of law, medicine, and engineering as well as liberal arts. The Johns Hopkins University, begun in 1876 under president Daniel Coit Gilman, at first had no undergraduate college at all but admitted only to the professional and graduate schools of a German type. In 1889 Clark University opened, under president G. Stanley Hall, as a graduate school of psychology. The year 1891 saw the west move into the field with Stanford University, led by an experimental ichthyologist, David Starr Jordan, and with sufficient money to employ the greatest scholars of the day. In this respect its main rival was the University of Chicago, re-established with the Rockefeller wealth and presided over by a great scholar of Hebrew, William Rainey Harper. While these new universities were coming into being, many of the older eastern colleges, such as Yale and Columbia, were also undergoing a gradual conversion to the university idea and form. By the beginning of the twentieth century the university was dominant in the American picture.

The last fifty years have seen tremendous growth in the size of the student bodies, from slightly over two hundred thousand to over two million students, of whom more than half are in our 121 universities, and less than a quarter in 453 separate liberal arts colleges. Many

1

of the largest universities are state institutions, but the largest of all is privately controlled and financed. Today the private liberal arts college has managed to hold its place by emphasizing the social and intellectual values of the intimate relations in a smaller student body. In curriculum and general educational philosophy, however, the universities still dominate the scene. And what are the major emphases which are now given in our American higher education? I should like to develop them under four main headings: culture, character, competence, and citizenship. The alliteration may help to tie them together.

The university of today is what it has been for seven centuries—a treasure house of culture. It is living proof that we are not the first who have trod this planet and that each age, race, nation, and outstanding individual has left some gift which we of today can make part of our own heritage. As Albert Einstein has told us, all things exist in a fourth dimension, of time; it is a function of education to help us to exist in time—in the riches of the past, the problems of the present, and the hopes of the future. We stand knee-deep in the river of human experience, knowing that much has flowed past before we came, that it continues on throughout our lives and probably will flow on in the future. It is this consciousness of our heritage from the past which sets man apart from the other members of the animal kingdom; in many ways the bees and the ants may be our social superiors, but in this respect they have not developed. Because this heritage is what glorifies the human being, it is well that we call its study the "humanities."

A university operates upon at least three levels—instruction, research, and services. In the area of the humanities the purpose of instruction is to enable the student to enter into his cultural inheritance. This can be achieved by the student partly through absorption, partly through creation. He can absorb the experience of history, the wisdom of philosophy, and the vicarious emotions and adventures of literature through reading. Through the techniques of teaching, students can be trained to read rapidly, accurately, and with critical appreciation. During the early stages the books can be prescribed or recommended by the faculty, so that the best of our cultural heritage will be known; but as the student gains maturity, he should be given more and more freedom of choice.

At times I fear that reading for enjoyment has become one of the lost arts. Children have so many other forms of recreation to compete for their time—sports in the afternoons, television in the evenings, trips on the week ends—that they have little opportunity to establish the reading habit. I recall happily the rainy afternoons and the long evenings which I spent reading through all the children's books on the shelves of the branch library near my home. On my twelfth birthday I received gifts in the form of cash, which I carried proudly to the downtown secondhand bookstore and invested, after a day of browsing, in a twenty-volume complete set of Sir Walter Scott and a thirty-volume complete set of Charles Dickens. And during the next two years I read them all. When I was thirteen I secured an advertising pamphlet of the Globe-Wernicke Company entitled "The World's Best Books," and I was naïve enough to believe that it was my duty to read them all. Listed in the pamphlet were the titles of the "Harvard Classics"; and, since my father had the set in our library at home, I started with Volume I and proceeded on through the five-foot shelf. This was very heavy reading for a teenager, but I plowed ahead, often without comprehension; this is why I say that the immature reader should be helped in his selection of books. On the other hand, I built up the habit of voluminous reading which has stood me in good stead all my life. Of course, some of the books were trivial, such as Horatio Alger's success stories or the adventures of Tom Swift, Frank Merriwell, and the Rover Boys; but I learned many of the facts of history from Henty and Joseph Altsheler, and they led me on to Stevenson, Dumas, Hugo, Thackeray, and others of high quality. When I arrived at college, the habit of reading was so ingrained that I dropped in every day for an hour in the Farnsworth Room of the Widener Library and read my way straight through the beautifully bound sets of Clemens, Shaw, and Galsworthy. To this day I can resist the blandishments of radio and television if I can have a good book waiting in my study, and I thank my lucky stars that I was allowed to become an ardent reader when I was a child. I suppose it is never too late to mend, and our college education should give every encouragement to leisure reading, but it is best if begun early. It has been said that the best university is a collection of books, and certainly the college library provided the gold mine in which the students, aided by the faculty, can dig for the riches of our civilization.

Although our culture is largely contained in books, it is also in music and art and must be heard and seen. Higher education must provide opportunities for listening to the best in music and drama, and in sufficient quantities to make a lasting impression. Perhaps radio's chief contribution to our civilization is the tremendous rise in music appreciation which it has brought about. If color television can do the same service for our appreciation of painting and its allied arts, may the day be hastened.

But it is not well enough that we teach enjoyment; we must teach the skills of creation as well. The creative technique of philosophy is meditation and thought; of literature it is writing; of music it is singing or playing an instrument or composing; of dramatics it is acting; of the graphic and plastic arts it is drawing and painting and sculpture. "What!" exclaims the skeptic, "are we expected to make accomplished artists in a dozen fields?" Of course not. But G. K. Chesterton, in one of his characteristic paradoxes, advised "Whatever is worth doing is worth doing poorly." By this I take him to mean that even though we may never acquire any real skill, we should try our hand at a number of creative tasks, in order that we may truly appreciate art when it is well done. And in the process we may at least learn to write clear and effective English prose. Ability to write correctly in one's own native tongue is a cultural goal which we have a right to demand of every college graduate.

So far I have spoken only of the instructional function of a university in the humanities. The faculty in these departments must also carry on research into our cultural heritage, to provide new light upon the past. For many years, under the powerful influence of the new sciences, research in the humanities aped the scientific techniques and jargon, and nothing was acceptable unless it was "philology" or "archeology" or "musicology." Today, however, there is a strong interest in rhetorical analysis, aesthetic criticism, and examination of art in artistic terms. Some of our graduate schools are permitting students to present a novel or play or symphony in place of the traditional doctoral research dissertation. Faculty members of our universities are expected to work in our research libraries and studios and to direct other workers in the production of books and paintings and operas, which, in turn, become a part of our cultural heritage.

The service function of the university to the humanities is carried on by the university library or libraries, by the museums, and by the public performances of theater, orchestra, or chorus. Administrators are accustomed to hear groans about the high expense of adding thousands of books each year to the libraries or of maintaining museums, with their manifold services; but how can a university become a true treasure house of culture if it has neither books nor artifacts? We will all agree that, particularly in our larger cities, students and faculty should make use of the agencies of culture which exist away from the campus, and the university should supplement rather than merely duplicate. The colleges of New York City, for example, can never hope to rival the collection of the Metropolitan Museum of Art or the music of the Philharmonic and the Metropolitan Opera or the professional theater of Broadway; therefore, they should bring their students in touch with the best where it is and spend their own funds to develop other areas.

The cultural function of higher education has been central for seven centuries; the same is true of its purpose as a builder and strengthener of character. The earliest universities were established as an arm of the church; a major reason was the preparation of a learned clergy. Religion was taken for granted as the binding element in all education. When the first American colleges were founded and for many years thereafter, the presidents were ordained ministers, who presided over the daily worship services, taught the required Senior course in Christian ethics, and looked to the healthful spiritual growth of every student. The entire atmosphere of the college was such that it assumed that the character of the individual would be strengthened by living there for four years.

The growing secularization of our universities during the past century has shifted the focus upon character development from a religious to a psychological center. Instead of piety and self-sacrifice, we now talk of self-realization, self-fulfilment, self-reliance, self-respect and self-government (in the personal rather than the political sense). Yet there is dissatisfaction with a merely biological interpretation of individual differences. As Dean Theodore Blegen said recently at a conference in Albany, "Man is not a blood-powered adjunct to a tractor." In their recent report on preparation for medical school in liberal arts colleges, Deans Severinghaus, Carman, and Cadbury applauded a growing "concern for moral values . . . personal and social responsibility . . . ethical and moral problems . . . service to one's fellow man." The question is: What can the college do about character?

Liberal education is by definition the education of free men, preparation for freedom. But freedom has no meaning unless man has a choice, and when we make a choice we exercise our sense of values. Professor George Counts, in his recent book, *Education and American Civilization*, states the issue thus:

The essence of any civilization is found in its values, in its preferences, its moral commitments, its esthetic judgments, its deepest loyalties, its conception of the good life, its standards of excellence, its measures of success, its teachings regarding the things for which and by which men should live, and, if need be, die. The issue at stake in the coming years is nothing less than the birth, the death, and the survival of values.

The character of a man, therefore, might be said to be determined by his set of values. Differences in personality have always demanded an explanation from the scholars, from the theory of the medieval physiologists of the four humors—red blood or *sanguis*, if dominant, makes the sanguine, cheerful, healthy man; phlegm in excess makes him phlegmatic, apathetic, sluggish; yellow bile, or *choler*, makes a man choleric, irascible, wrathful; and black bile, or *melan choler*, brings on melancholy, dejection, gloom —down to the Freudian types and the Gestalt of modern psychology.

The idea that personality and character are determined by the value-pattern suggests a possible function for education at the university level. Let us provide a character H-bomb to offset the military H-bomb now terrifying the earth. Perhaps society will be helped if our graduates can be taught honesty, humility, humanity, and humor in college classrooms. The study of mathematics, experiments in the laboratory, the taking of examinations, should convince us that cheating robs only ourselves; as Polonius told Laertes, "To thine own self be true, and it must follow as the night the day, thou canst not then be false to any man."

Humility or lack of conceit should come from a realization of our ignorance. Let us assume that a student entering the university has knowledge equivalent to a circle with diameter X; at every point on the circumference of that circle he should be conscious of an area of ig-

norance outside the circle. Four years later we hope the circle he knows has grown to diameter $2X$; but the circumference has also doubled, and his admission of ignorance should be increased. The man who knows the most, the great scholar, should be the most humble because he is most conscious of the areas of the unknown.

By "humanity" I mean consideration of the effects of what we do upon others. Christianity preaches that the individual human soul is the highest value in the sight of God, democracy that the individual human being and his rights take precedence over the superstate. Sympathy with the hopes and troubles of others becomes a virtue when it leads to the alleviation of suffering.

When I ask for humor as a character trait, I am seeking not for the comic cutup or the senseless giggler but for the ability to see life in its proper proportions, to recognize incongruity, and to help restore balance and sanity, often with the sauce of a kindly smile. We Americans have great respect for these good-humor men, the Mark Twains and the Will Rogerses, for they help to give us character as a nation. The careful study of literature, both tragedy and comedy, should help us develop both humanity and humor.

The old college curriculum combined instruction in the humanities with indoctrination in the principles of morality and character. Latin and Greek gave ample excuse for philosophy, and every event in history offered a problem in ethics. Culture and character, therefore, have gone hand in hand. Research at the universities in character has, however, been little developed. The only departments to interest themselves have been religion and psychology, and much of their research has been tangential. Here is an area of great opportunity. Psychiatry deals with the pathology of character, and educational psychology has limited itself too strictly to the elementary and secondary levels. We need research in the growth of character among mature normal men and women.

The early college contented itself with a curriculum built chiefly around culture and character. Actual training for the professions of medicine and law was secured by "reading" in a doctor's or lawyer's office. But during the second quarter of the nineteenth century engineering and law and medicine began to establish schools and curriculums, and eventually many of these schools became affiliated with universities. Normal schools grew into teachers' colleges; the Morrill Act of 1862 set up schools of agriculture, mostly in connection with state colleges and universities; and during the past century there has been a steady growth in the number and size of "professional" schools of business, pharmacy, music, journalism, nursing, architecture, forestry, veterinary medicine, osteopathy, optometry, dentistry, social work, and library science. All these occupations now call themselves "professions" because their vocational training is given at the college or postcollege level, but the educational program prescribed for the degree is designed not so much for culture or character as for competence. If we engage a dentist to work on our teeth or an architect to build our house, we may be happy to know that he is steeped in the literary and artistic heritage of the human race, and we hope that he is honest and humane, but we insist that he know the techniques of his trade.

The medieval curriculum of grammar, logic, rhetoric, arithmetic, geometry, music, and astronomy was constructed for the needs of a leisure-class society and the priesthood. Today America really has no leisure class, though we all may be striving to reach that level on retirement. In this country we expect every man or woman to pull his own weight in the boat, regardless of inherited wealth. Every man works for self-respect, even if he does not need to work for a living. The sons of John D. Rockefeller, Jr., provide an excellent example of Americans at work. With such an emphasis upon competence at some useful occupation, it is natural that vocational programs should dominate higher education. Of the approximately 500,000 degrees granted in the United States in 1950, only 150,000 were in the liberal arts; the other 350,000 were earned in professional schools at the undergraduate and graduate levels. And it would be safe to say that most of the degrees in liberal arts were intended for use as tickets of admission to business or teaching or scientific work or home economics or to graduate schools.

Certainly there is nothing low or venial in vocational motivation. Educators should welcome motivation to study, almost without regard to source. The vision of a professional diploma at the end may carry the student through many a subject which in itself has little intrinsic interest for him. Even if the vocational drive lasts for only a short time, it may perform a valuable function—especially if it is succeeded by another and stronger drive. Many a student shifts his sights from one profession to another, particularly during his undergraduate career, and there is no harm done; actually, his education is probably broader as a result.

In the area of vocational and professional competence, the university has many functions. First of all, it helps to select and sift the suitable candidates for the various professions. Tests of vocational interest and aptitude have been developed to a point where they are very helpful, but they must be supplemented by academic records, general mental ability tests, and personal interviews. Certain professional schools are much stiffer in their entrance requirements than others, partly because the profession places an arbitrary limitation on numbers. Some professions demand from two to four years of liberal arts training before admission to the study of the craft, whereas others include the training in the undergraduate years. The logic of these differentiations is sometimes hard to perceive.

In the teaching of the professions, the question is constantly asked: Can a man be a good teacher without also being a good practitioner? The desire to combine theory with practice has led to a considerable movement back and forth between the classroom and the professional office. In medical schools, for example, only a few members of the clinical faculty are full-time teachers, and these few practice medicine or surgery in order that they may show to the students the latest techniques. Many teachers in the business school or engineering school spend a day or two each week and their summer vacations with a corporation on a retainer basis. If held within reasonable bounds, this practice should be encouraged. Sabbatical years are frequently used to refresh the professor's acquaintance with the harsh facts of the "world outside." Members of the profession, through their guild organizations, are inclined to demand a share in the planning of the curriculum and in the accrediting of the schools themselves. This has produced some upgrading of faculty and teaching but has also

proved a millstone around the neck of the universities; there is a strong movement under way to simplify and unify the whole accrediting process.

It is in the professions, the field of competence, that the research function of the universities has mushroomed to fantastic proportions. In at least two great engineering colleges the budget for research exceeds the entire budget for the remainder of the institution; and a similar proportion or lack of proportion prevails in the budgets of medical schools, colleges of agriculture, and departments of physics or chemistry. In 1950, over $222,000,000 was spent on organized research, mostly in the sciences. Now that the federal government has discovered the research abilities of university faculties, most of this research money comes from Washington. The recently established National Science Foundation is merely another step in the same direction. Even the private foundations show a preference for the professional schools when they make grants for investigations. And it must be admitted that this constant stimulus from public and private sources has produced amazing results. Most of the recent Nobel prize winners in science have been university professors, and our medical schools have produced some of the magical cures of our day.

In like manner, university services are also very heavy in the professional fields. University hospitals, medical clinics for diagnosis and treatment, short refresher courses for business executives or teachers, practicing law institutes, and the burgeoning enterprise of adult education and extension courses have become an important part of many universities. Just as Uncle Sam has found universities helpful, so the professional men desire to maintain a continuing relationship of mutual assistance with their own or the nearest school. This can be built into a healthy relationship for both.

Culture, character, competence—and, finally, citizenship. Once it was assumed that literacy was all that is required for good citizenship, but today we realize that propaganda works twice as effectively on those who can read. There are no more desert islands where we can escape from the world's problems, no Brigadoons which can remain unchanged for a century while the earth rolls on. When Andrei Vishinsky, in an address to the United Nations Assembly, asserted that communism would win the world, not with bombs and industrial production, but with the idea and inspiring concept of a communist society, he was hurling a challenge to the universities of the Western world. Can we teach our people to believe ardently in our democratic social philosophy, which places individual man and his rights at the heart of America, and at the same time to work with and for our republican form of government, with the checks of legislative and judicial and executive branches and the balances of federal and state and local community responsibilities? Have we the faith for survival?

Our colleges can and must teach good citizenship in part in the classroom. By the study of history, from the Greek city-states to contemporary America, we can teach how man has gradually won his freedoms from the oppressors. In economics we can show how nineteenth-century free enterprise, with its pitfalls of exploitation and monopoly, has in twentieth-century America evolved "past socialism and communism," in the phrase of Frederick Lewis Allen, to an economy characterized by the desire for service to the public, a

rising standard of living, widely distributed ownership of corporations, and the channeling of wealth back into society through foundations such as the Rockefeller, Carnegie, Ford, Mellon, Kellogg, or Kresge. In our courses in political science we can reveal how the American Constitution has been tested in wars and peace for one hundred and sixty-five years and has proved flexible and durable beyond any other. Governor Thomas Dewey in a recent speech insisted that our schools should see that every student knows where the strategic materials of the world are located, what government controls them, and why America must keep a world of friends. Yes, in our classrooms our university faculties can teach geopolitics and foreign languages as a channel of understanding, and all the social sciences, like sociology and anthropology and social psychology, can contribute to our understanding and faith in democratic republicanism.

But this is not enough. Recent experience in various parts of the world has proved painfully that learning to live in freedom is a slow process and cannot be taught from books. To produce graduates with a belief in democracy, our universities must themselves be filled with the democratic spirit. To prepare men and women to debate and argue on public issues, we must encourage debate and free discussion on the campus. As Mark Van Doren pointed out recently, children cannot be convinced by argument; this is a characteristic of mature minds, and universities must bring about the steady maturing of student minds. Much of this maturing must be emotional rather than rational; our universities must help students find safe and positive outlets for their emotions, must cultivate sympathy with the emotions of others, and, above all, must lead to a mature control of the emotions by the intellect, so that our feelings aid rather than destroy our judgment. It has often been said that man is unfit to govern others until he can govern himself. If life on our campuses is democratic, the foreign students studying here by the thousands will take back to their native lands something of the flavor of democratic living. In like manner, travel abroad can do much to give Americans perspective on their own civilization.

Research into the problems of American economics and into the complexities of public administration provides another challenge to higher education. During political campaigns the words "brain trust" may be used by the party out of power with vituperative effect, but no national administration today can possibly function without the expert services of economists and other social scientists from university faculties. It is just and right that our universities should be service stations for the nation.

In like manner, universities become the civic centers for their communities. Professors are the consultants to municipal bureaus and state officials. The college buildings house public meetings and forums where important issues are discussed. The more the university builds itself into the life of the city, state, and nation, the more truly it is performing its proper function. If the Gothic cathedral was the flower of the Middle Ages, can we not hope that the American college is the flower of modern America?

Culture, character, competence, and citizenship as the objectives of the modern university combine the best of the old and the new—and that has been the dream of the teacher since the dawn of civilization.

THE RELATIONSHIP BETWEEN THE LIBRARY
AND COLLEGIATE OBJECTIVES

R. F. ARRAGON

A QUARTER-century of membership in a college-library committee has given me, as a layman coming before a conference of professionals, some assurance and much caution. I have been close to problems of book budget and departmental allocation, of reserve books, documents, shelving, staffing, and of the blueprint for a library wing, at least close enough to recognize their complexity and to respect the difficulties of those who have to deal with them day after day, year in and year out. I am hesitant, therefore, about putting my topic in the form of "What are we college professors now asking of the college library?" suspecting that perhaps it had better be "What opportunities do the curriculum and the extra-curricular interests of students now offer to libraries?" May we on either side of the professional line try to answer both questions at once?

Changing collegiate objectives or at least changing methods of achieving these have given or offered the library an increasingly strategic place in the education of the undergraduate. This has not been primarily because of the development of programs in general education, with their aim to provide a broad and common intellectual experience at the college level (or earlier), but rather because of the efforts to engage students actively in learning for themselves. Lectures, textbooks, and examinations have been supplemented and, though seldom entirely replaced, have been in many curriculums overshadowed by methods of challenging students to take a large share in their education. If in the natural sciences this has long been sought in the laboratories (when not reduced to routine), in the humanities and social sciences it has more recently been encouraged by transforming recitation or quiz section into group discussion. Discussion requires something to be discussed, something which students can try to understand for themselves, raise questions and hazard answers about, and point to as evidence for or against these answers. What serves on the group-conference table as an object of discussion can often be equally the object of individual interpretation in essays or reports.

Usually this object is a book or part of a book (other possibilities will be referred to later), not one that needs only be memorized (like many textbooks) but one that calls for imagination and inquiry—a poem, drama, or novel, a history, an essay in criticism or in philosophy, a treatise in one of the social sciences. When the purpose is the cultivation of sensitivity and reflection, of analysis and judgment, rather than the inculcation of information and ready-made conclusions, the teacher and student can —indeed, must—cut through the devices that protect them from thought and emotion and have recourse to books that encourage them to think and to feel for themselves. They go to the sources, primary and secondary, where they may encounter originality in ideas and in expression. The return to the sources is particularly noticeable in the humanities, for original written works are among their characteristic objects of study. Generalizations as formulas for the understanding of life or of art are not their aim, or at least their primary aim, nor is it the classification and summary of writers and writings. These staples of textbooks, when useful, are so as helps for approaching the works, not as substitutes for them. Introductory and other essays by sensitive and critical scholars, essays which are themselves objects worthy of humanistic study, will contribute more than will outlines and commonplaces. The aim of the humanities is the engagement of the feeling and thought of the student in the written (or other) word before him. It is upon this that his appreciation and understanding are focused and through this that they are developed.

The humanistic emphasis upon reading and interpretation applies not only to works of poetic and prose fiction and of literary criticism but to histories and to all written evidences, both literary and documentary, of particular events, persons, and situations in the past. It applies to the works of a philosopher, to the exposition of a theory in the natural sciences, and to an essay or systematic treatise in the social sciences. All these may be studied for themselves as humanistic events, that is, as particular expressions of men's thought. Emphasis upon the use of books other than textbooks is not confined, however, to the humanities. Philosophy and the social sciences as fields that aim at generalization and system-building can challenge their students to imaginative and critical inquiry by confronting them with examples of such inquiry. Here, as in the humanities, it is by analysis and interpretation of particular creations of human thought that the stu-

dent in group discussion and in writing essays and reports under guidance educates himself.

No longer dependent upon a handy manual which, with some lecture notes, will assure passing examinations and getting a grade in a course, the student must have access to a wide variety of printed materials. The number and range of these may be illustrated, in an extreme but not untypical form, from the humanities course at Reed College. The poetic works used in this two-year program include epics as diverse as the *Odyssey*, Lucretius' *On the Nature of Things*, the *Song of Roland* and the *Divine Comedy*, a romance of Chrétien de Troyes, some of the *Canterbury Tales*, and lyrics ranging from the seventeenth century to the twentieth. Dramatic poetry from the Greeks to Goethe has an important part. The novel is introduced (or anticipated) with *Don Quixote* and is a major concern from Stendhal to Kafka. Philosophy, especially as political, social, and ethical theory, has representatives from Plato to Dewey. Specifically Christian writing is drawn from the New Testament, Augustine, Thomas Aquinas, Luther, Pascal, and others. The works of Herodotus and Thucydides are matched by those of modern historians. These, which offer the background of institutional history for the major phases of Western society, are varied. Special volumes and chapters, wherever possible those of thoughtful specialists, are preferred to chronological surveys.

The range is not so wide in most programs in the humanities and the social sciences, but the practice is often similar and is becoming increasingly so, especially in the introductory and general courses. The resulting problem for the student of getting hold of so many and diverse works is serious. He can scarcely be expected to buy all or a large proportion of them. A common solution is to find or to put the materials into a volume or two. Anthologies published for the general reader as well as for the student are likely to contain whole works and, in consequence, to be limited to special kinds or periods of literature. Discursive subject matter, such as political theory and art criticism, can rarely be represented in anthologies with complete treatises, but long and continuous sections from a few authors may serve well. The inclusion of selections from many works necessarily cuts down the excerpts from each work to the point where they are likely to illustrate what the editor wanted them to say rather than how the author developed his thought. Continuity is better than spotty coverage; a full chapter than paragraphs from several chapters; a sequence of chapters than isolated ones. Much depends, of course, on the nature of the work.

Poetry is difficult to cut, even in the case of epics, though there may be sections that have enough structural distinctness to be usable alone, with the aid of lectures or introductions suggesting their place in the whole. The *Divine Comedy* is at least a debatable example. Lyric poetry and drama are denatured by cutting. Novels sometimes may be reduced without too much loss (witness Putnam's editing of the portable Cervantes), but not to the extent required for anthologies. Short stories would be better for this purpose. Histories lose much if read in short sections, unless we want only speeches from Thucydides or tales from Herodotus. For modern historians, the alternative of selecting short historical articles from journals or of commissioning special essays for a collaborative volume has not yet proved a definite success, at least in our experience. Docu-

ments (charters, laws, letters, etc.) can be anthologized, though cutting is a delicate matter. It may, as with other kinds of materials, doctor the evidence.

A similar distortion may result from an introduction to the excerpts chosen from any author. More frequent and therefore more serious is the hindrance to the student's reading of the passages for himself that may result from telling him in advance what he is to find. He often needs some background, but how definitely directive should it be? Recent collections of documents have been organized so that the materials could be used to throw light on particular historical and theoretical problems and even to answer specific questions posed by the editors. Such organization provides a unifying frame of reference that sharpens and narrows the students' interpretation of diverse selections. Like laboratory experiments and mathematical problems, it trains in certain skills of analysis and has its place along with other methods of handling original materials; but it may, especially outside the purely documentary field, so limit self-directed and open-minded exploration as to do more harm than good. Indication of relevant points of view or of alternative and controversial meanings may, on occasion, encourage a student to vary or to enlarge his own perspective. When we want to do more than to train specific skills, the indication of a documentary problem, like the introduction to selections from literary, historical, or philosophical works, should be suggestive rather than prescriptive, opening up rather than foreclosing the issues.

Anthologies, at their best usable for specific purposes, do not solve the general problem. Even if a course staff can make its own collection (and what staff can be satisfied with that of some other college?) and has a wide margin of tolerance as to length of fragments, an anthology cannot be inclusive enough. Works that are to be read in full will bulk too large, and others will be too few (for an extensive course) or too scantily represented. Attractive translations will be protected by copyright. Moreover, even one's own anthology constrains the flexibility of the program, inhibiting the innovative enthusiasm of a teacher or a staff for fresh and more fruitful materials. Anthologies of various sorts may be used to supplement one another and to supplement the use of separate volumes containing one or a few closely related complete works, upon which, as far as possible, reliance should be placed. These are, to my mind, the best solution, one that has become more practical with the multiplication of series (several of them inexpensive) of literary, historical, and philosophical classics and of contemporary writings in the same and related fields. They are a boon to the teacher and the student and to the college library.

For the library has been and is likely to continue to be primarily responsible for providing the duplicates necessary in courses that do not rely on textbooks and anthologies and seek to take the student to original works in as close to the original form as possible. The duplicate reserve collection is older than programs in general education, even older than the attention, begun about thirty-five years ago, to "great books" (any required or attractive course that strayed occasionally beyond a textbook or two in its assignments needed a reserve); but the popularity of the use of primary materials, combined with the movement for general education, has forced the extension of the number of these collections and their expansion in size and scope. I wonder, however, whether even now they

are adequate to the needs, actual and potential. In so far as they are not so, the reasons are obvious.

The difficulties are probably at bottom largely financial. One to four or five is certainly not high for the ratio of copies to students, even when many members of the class buy a considerable proportion of the works assigned. The ratio might advantageously be made better than that for a book that alone comprises the reading for a single week. To spend any part of limited book budgets on duplicate copies when it might go toward increasing the new resources of the library seems well-nigh criminal to librarians and professors alike, and I share this feeling. Special funds are preferable, either granted from tuition receipts or (what comes to the same) an over-all book fee charged to each student, perhaps as part of a broader incidental fee covering laboratory materials as well. Rental, with private purchase as an alternative for the student, will also cover costs in several years, but seems of doubtful practicability except for a few volumes to be read steadily over a number of weeks or months and to be kept on the assignment lists until paid for. A collection does not have to be bought all at once, but it should never be considered as completed. Funds must be available for continued experimentation with new books, to fill gaps, to replace unsuccessful readings, to put in better translations, better editions, and more up-to-date secondary works, and, in general, to effect changes in the pattern and emphasis of the course. The available reading must not be frozen, if the course and its staff are to stay alive.

Book purchase, as I need not tell you, is only the beginning of the problems. The cost of cataloging and of removal may be kept down by accessioning only one copy of each book. More important is shelf room both for the changing active reserve and for the far larger duplicate reserve pool. The duplicate collection at Reed (a college of about six hundred) numbers over 10,000 books, or 10 per cent of a total book collection (exclusive of public documents) of just over 100,000. Even a lower percentage will cause difficulties, in view of the normal slightness of the unused margin of shelf space for expansion, and of the continual and, it seems to me, inevitable increase in the regular collections. Space for books is expensive, and the competition for it keen. More serious still is the staff time required for the servicing of the duplicate reserves. The assignment of different works every week or fortnight means the continual rotation of books on the active reserve shelves and would, I should suppose, complicate the rental as much as, if not more than, it does the overnight loan system. Unless rented, copies must be available for continuous use during the day, both for individual students and for group conferences; many of them will be charged out in the late afternoon, others kept for the evening (perhaps in special desk-reserve) and charged out at closing time; all must be checked in again in the morning.

The cost of staff for reserve circulation can be kept to a minimum by student self-service in checking out books from open reserve shelves. There will be some misuse of the privilege (the amount varying with local habits and student self-governing morale) and the irrecoverable loss of a few copies each year. The cost of staffing closed active reserve shelves (and thereby probably also the inactive reserves) is, however, in our experience far greater than that of replacing the losses. The size of our problem at Reed can be suggested by the overnight reserve circulation of 50,000 volumes for the academic year of nine months (1953–54), excluding daytime use and the use of the departmental libraries of the natural sciences (the latter an important item in a college having a high proportion of natural-science majors), for both of which we have no figures. The overnight reserve circulation in the humanities and social sciences averaged about 300 per weeknight and over 80 per student throughout the year. The intensity of use may be illustrated by the result of a brief study of the signatures on the cards of sample reserve books in a relatively large Sophomore course. These covered daytime as well as overnight use. Ninety per cent of the class checked out practically all these books with regularity.

This circulation and its problems are not confined to general courses and duplicate copies. Advanced courses in the humanities and social sciences also are sending students to a variety of primary and secondary sources for class discussion, reports, and papers. The needs may include duplicate copies for some key works, such as philosophic treatises used for common interpretation around the discussion table, but often reach beyond these to standard, provocative, and recent special studies or monographs on the particular matters under consideration. Common problems rather than common reading unify the discussions, and all the participants may thereby get some acquaintance with many of the significant works in the field. Familiarity with them and comparative evaluation of them are greatly facilitated by the chance to handle and to sample all the books in use for the course. Accessible shelves again seem called for, and, indeed, not only for books temporarily withdrawn from the general collection for reserve but for that collection itself.

There are many technical factors involved in the problems of open stacks and open reserves that will occur to librarians more readily than to a layman—budgets, staff organization, pattern of library space both for shelves and for reading, size of student body and of collections, reshelving by staff rather than by students, and the like. Reserves may be open and not the stacks, or vice versa. A reserve reading-room may have open shelves, with a checkup on students leaving it as a practical compromise between freedom and security, though this goes against the grain of my educational principles. Special departmental rooms may be made available to the undergraduate majors or by special permission to undergraduates engaged in a reading or research project. Small colleges have, to my mind, a distinct advantage in the practicability of making their collections open to all students. The effectiveness of free use of the stacks and of the reserves can be heightened by tables and cubicles to facilitate browsing and study. Reference advice can suggest where and how to find books on one's subject and what books and articles may possibly be helpful, but not usually, I should think, exactly what to read. Special guidance is obviously needed in the location of materials in public documents. Careful introduction of entering students is particularly important, introduction to the layout of the stacks and of the reserves as well as to the card catalog, circulation practices, and reference shelves. These services are in line with the general educational policy of encouraging students from the beginning to know and to use good books.

In spite of the difficulties and costs, the reason for having a college library is the furtherance of student self-education, and the college should recognize the rele-vant services as a necessary charge upon it for making possible the kind of education that it believes in and promises to offer. Undergraduates are no longer simply pupils, and the possibilities for intellectual initiative (which indeed should begin before college) should not be postponed to the graduate school or even to the Senior year.

Before examining further the nature of the collection on the open shelves and the purchase policy that determines it, we should have in view another aspect of the contemporary trend in college programs. Beyond general education and the more specialized seminar-like advanced courses lies undergraduate research. Perhaps the most recent evidence of this concern is in the establishment of undergraduate grants in the "behavioral sciences" through the Social Science Research Council for the summer after the Junior year. Independent, or individual, reading done under supervision through private conferences and written reports might be added as a fourth category; but the relationship of this practice to the service of the library is not different from that of the upper-class course, unless it is so focused on a particular problem that it becomes in effect a project in research. Research by the undergraduate, whether done for a serious paper in an advanced course, for a special project or reading course, for honors work or a Bachelor's thesis required of all graduates, is intended to further some of the same ends as class discussion based on challenging reading materials. In a more specialized and individual way it should encourage critically responsible inquiry and the capacity through analysis to formulate and to support conclusions. It must necessarily relate to a particular topic, usually in a special departmental field and connected with a major program, but this does not make it unsuitable for liberal education, unless it is done as a technical exercise that does not stretch the mind and give it the sense of discovery. Inquiry directed at a particular problem may be more liberalizing than an unimaginative, though broader, course.

Undergraduate research, however, reinforces the demands made by the seminar type of advanced course in major fields upon the specialized resources of the college library. The standard works, good recent monographs, novel and fruitful interpretations, and scholarly editions of basic texts make essential contributions to many a class and provide the necessary background also for the pursuit of a problem in research. A few specialized journals should be on hand for occasional articles and, more important, for book reviews and bibliographical surveys. The student should become at least familiar with what these are and how they can serve both in exploratory reading in a field and in specific inquiry.

Thus far I can probably go without much question, in spite of the cost of a purchase policy that would insure even a modest approach to such an ideal. We may grant that we ought to try to achieve this, even when we fear that we cannot adequately do so. I have, however, mentioned only secondary sources and basic original texts (literary, philosophical, historical, and other classics). Occasional supplement to the library's collection of these works may be made, when necessary for a particular project, such as a Senior thesis, by interlibrary loan or by special purchase. But what of primary materials other than the texts of classics? Do we need and can we afford, in the library of a small college, documents, statistical data, letters, old newspapers and other sources that challenge the inquirer in a way that the comparison

of secondary authorities, however useful this may be, cannot do? Students of literature, philosophy, historiography, and social theory may, at the undergraduate level, find good, annotated texts sufficient for their projects; but inquiry into institutional history, economic behavior, political and sociological problems, and biography and related fields will be deficient in its value, even as a trial run, without opportunity to interpret at least a sample of firsthand data. Such an opportunity cannot be offered in every part of every field; but perhaps the need can be met by the gradual purchase of some key materials in special areas. History sources, for example, might be collected for one or two English centuries, for a period in American diplomatic or constitutional history, for local or regional history. Care on the part of faculty and of library staff in planning and in watching for opportune purchase of sets will make small funds accomplish much over a number of years in carrying out a modest program.

For the social sciences, United States documents are a mine, and fortunate is the library that is a selective depository, even though this good fortune brings its problems—carefully planned selection, continuous checking of what is received against what is published, listing and filing, search in aid of a student or of a faculty supervisor of a student project, and so on. I need not demonstrate that these tasks require at least one full-time, well-trained, and experienced librarian; as a member of a division of history and social science, I can assure you that in the service given to undergraduate research he is worth the cost. Microfilms and microcards will increasingly add to available research materials, though they, too, require special techniques, equipment, and space for handling.

Books in foreign languages outside of the language departments offer a controversial issue for small undergraduate libraries, one that is probably more and more decided in the negative. The choice is in effect between a good work in English and a good, perhaps a better, one in French or German (less usually in Italian, Spanish, or Russian). The original may sometime be translated; but when will this be, and may the work not in some cases be vital now? Few students (and they may be becoming rarer) can, and fewer still will, read it. Some may note it on the shelf and wish that they could read it. I continue to think that the library and the faculty should do something for the few, if only as a protest against our national monolinguality; but I suspect that we can do little more than set an occasional example of a principle. Only university libraries can make a rule of maintaining fully satisfactory collections of significant secondary works (to say nothing of source materials) in modern European languages, at least outside their literatures.

In the maintenance of a good collection, faculty members are likely to have themselves as well as the students in mind, as, for instance, in the purchase of books in foreign languages, if they are not also afflicted by inability to read them. Self-interest is a danger when it is narrowed to a specialty; but, if the faculty know and like worth-while books and have broad interests, they may be ordering to help both themselves and the students to keep abreast of what is being done in the variety of fields that they may touch in departmental and interdepartmental courses in a small college.

The steady and wide use of imaginative and thought-provoking books as instruments of education should, we hope, direct the interest of undergraduates beyond the completion of the assignment. If curricular and library services encourage firsthand acquaintance with creative and scholarly works through group discussion and individual inquiry and through open shelves and convenient arrangements for reading in and out of the library, we should anticipate, if we are doing these things well, not only an increase in ability to read perceptively, imaginatively, and discriminatingly but also curiosity, enjoyment, and excitement in reading and in having books to read. Concrete evidence of habits of reading and of book purchase derived from such instruction rather than simply from textbooks and anthologies of fragmentary source materials and from lectures and examinations are hard for me to come by. I can make only a suggestion or two.

A college bookstore may be a barometer of the amount and character of student purchase. Thus, at Reed, a student body of 600 (of which about 230 are Freshmen) bought this spring 125 portable Cervantes when this was put on the reading list for the course in Freshman humanities. The student purchase was in the face of the library purchase of fifty copies, but was apparently as much because of, as in spite of, the duplicate reserve. Upper-classmen and Freshmen decided that they wanted their own copies of an attractive book. It could not, indeed, as I have already said, have been put on the required list for so general and inclusive a course without library provision. From many years' experience we have concluded that library service does not dissuade students from building up their own libraries. The reverse is the case in courses in which the student is not required to buy books. The sale of literary, philosophical, and historical classics is large and steady. It is highest for Freshmen and Seniors. The score of the latter, who buy more books than does any other class, and that of Juniors, too, is enhanced by standard scholarly works and up-to-date monographs. This happy situation would not be possible without the enterprise of the manager of the bookstore, but his enterprise is in the way he takes advantage of the emphasis of the curriculum and collaborates in purchasing for the library as well as for the store.

How much students borrow from the library for other than course reading I do not know. The 20,000 volumes taken by 600 students each year in the regular four-week circulation (exclusive of the natural-science libraries) is probably in considerable part connected with courses and research projects, though a wide variety of books from the general collection is reserved from time to time for the use of advanced courses. There are signs, however, that, in spite of the pressure of assigned reading, students are attracted by the open shelves to look for other books, to become familiar with the resources of the library in various fields, and to charge out some of the books they find. Do curricular and extra-curricular reading habits continue after college? A study made by the Reed librarian nearly a quarter of a century ago (when present methods were in use at the college, though not perhaps so intensively as now) suggests a favorable response.[1] I wish that I had a more recent one for the college and had been able to search for comparable studies made for other institutions. Fifty per cent of the graduates responded to the questionnaire, not quite equally divided between men and women, with an average (including some non-readers) of over ten hours per week of book reading for both professional and personal interests. Others can perhaps supply more convincing figures. The test would, of course, not be just how many and what books college graduates read but how they read these books and newspapers and periodicals as well, without our forgetting the results that ought to appear in how they think and feel and on what they base their interests and attitudes.

My discussion of the library's provision of books for curricular purposes has alluded to policies and facilities for their use, in particular in regard to access to and circulation of reserves and books in the main collection. I have assumed general or special reading-rooms ample for the daytime pressure and the possibility of relief by a one- or two-hour checkout for use outside the library before the time for overnight withdrawal. I have emphasized open shelves and suggested the pros and cons of self-help. Research also needs to be thought of in terms of convenience. Key sources for an individual project have to be kept together for several weeks or months, and related materials as well as dictionaries, encyclopedias, and other reference tools should be easily accessible. Desks in the stacks and rooms set aside for research, such as a Senior thesis room, are normal answers, though sometimes forgotten in the planning of small libraries.

Devices for encouragement of extra-curricular reading also have been common. Browsing-rooms with shelves of standard and recent literature or lounge-like comfort in a wing of a regular reading-room and strategically placed shelves for new accessions or for a rental collection of contemporary fiction, drama, poetry, and essays are examples that come readily to mind. Conveniently placed shelves or stands for current journals or

[1] Nell Unger, "Reading Interests and Habits of Reed College Alumni," *Reed College Bulletin*, Vol. X, No. 1 (January, 1931).

attractive and accessible periodical rooms may also further casual reading and the pursuit of special interests. Other methods as well are being tried on the initiative of librarians to lure undergraduates away from course assignments but not from books, a diversion to be applauded if it is effective in moderation. Whether it has been too successful or not successful enough and by what measure we should judge, I cannot say.

What more encouragement than facilities for getting books into the hands of students can libraries and librarians offer? Can they do anything on their own initiative to assist or to stimulate the faculty to make the library the center of study and of educational resources, at least in the humanities and social sciences? (I am not in a position to resolve the problem presented in the natural sciences by the power of laboratories to draw books away from the central library into special libraries.) Librarians surely can collaborate with teachers in improving the book collections. They can make suggestions of purchases that will give better balance between areas in a field or will further departmental long-range plans for source materials or standard sets. They can call attention to new editions and translations and to new journals. To encourage the making of plans and to take some initiative in carrying them out may often be a delicate matter. It may take even greater tact to try to move a faculty and curriculum toward more reliance on the library and less on textbooks. The college librarian has more immediate acquaintance with the students' use of the collections than have most of the faculty members; but of greater importance for his influence is the *rapport* that he has established through his work with the faculty library committee and with individual teachers. He

is clearly in a stronger position if he is a member of the faculty and of faculty committees (as seems desirable) and stronger still if he does some teaching. In any case, with readiness to take advantage of local curricular studies and revisions, which have become numerous, librarians may be able to bore from within.

I have been speaking of books, the staple of libraries. More than books may, however, be expected of libraries. Now that programs in the history and interpretative analysis of art and music have become common, attention is given to provision for the firsthand acquaintance of students with works of the visual arts and of music. Libraries and art and music departments are natural alternatives and perhaps rivals for this responsibility.

"Firsthand acquaintance" may be considered euphemistic in two senses. Many students bring to the study of aesthetic objects little, if any, direct experience with the materials and tools of artistic creation; but this problem is scarcely one for the libraries. Closer to their concern is the normal need of substitutes for the originals either as visual objects or as performances. Modern technology has provided increasingly effective means of reproduction convenient for demonstration in lectures and for study by student groups and by individuals. After steel engravings came photographs and slides in black and white, and after these have come color prints and color slides. The last step is not recognized by all art historians as an advance; but, in spite of the vagaries of color reproductions, it seems to me that they awaken in the student at least an awareness that the qualities of painting are not limited to linear design and the plasticity of light and shadow. In music there is not the same degree of doubt that phonograph records are an improvement over the rolls for player pianos and that recording has improved. Whether or not everyone is agreed that long-playing records are more convenient for detailed analysis in class than the 78's, we shall evidently soon have to rely entirely on them, with the important exception that tape recording is developing as a competitor for certain teaching purposes. Teachers and librarians are not likely to overlook the place that recording has already taken also for presenting drama and poetry.

Collections of reproductions are not in themselves enough. Records need machines for playing them and scores and reference books for consultation. The presence of scores suggests the usefulness of a piano for some students. Histories of art, critical studies, and other works of reference are normally the accompaniments of a collection of photographs and prints in the visual arts, and I can imagine the value of a small projector and screen for more than lecture purposes. These facilities obviously call for special music and art rooms.

The problem of where these rooms should be located and under whose control arises from the several ends that they may have to serve in a small college. Students concentrating in the fine arts or in music will be constant users of the reproductions and of the reproducing machines, as will also the faculty of these departments. This active concern will attract the collections and equipment and at least some of the books to the departmental building or rooms. Students in nonspecialist courses in the liberal arts or general education program (including humanities courses) will be best served by central location and broad handling of the resources in art and music. Equally important are the interests of those who

wish to study and to enjoy paintings and music out of course. To serve them may seem at times to conflict with the convenience of both general and special courses and to warrant college supervision through the library.

These various services should be viewed as supplementary rather than competitive, and the same view applies to the alternatives of departmental and library provision and management. Attribution of responsibility to one or the other or to both would depend on the capacities and attitudes of the respective staffs, the available room space and the chances for increasing it, the convenience of location for the college as a whole, and the traditional strength and degree of success of the existing arrangement. The college is fortunate that has a library building of the size and plan that enable it to provide music and art rooms. The latter are, I suppose, more frequently housed there than are the former, for acoustical, if not for other, reasons; but it would seem wise in any case for the library to have some responsibility and supervision over what have become common resources for college education.

For circulation of art and music materials among students for private appreciation and study, the library appears to have definite advantage. It is better equipped than the average small department for charging out color prints, records, and scores. Framed color prints loaned by the term have proved popular at some institutions. A small rental charge has enabled us at Reed to purchase and to frame a growing collection. The long-playing record offers a similar opportunity, perhaps on a subscription basis, for revolving short loans when, as with prints, regular funds cannot be spared for additions and replacement.

The library is to be viewed as a storehouse of men's work of the past and the present or rather of the various records of that work. This includes creation in stone and in steel, in pigment and in clay, in tone and in rhythm, as well as in words in the books with which this paper has been largely concerned. To help to make all these available is the challenge to the college library offered by the broadening scope of college programs and at the same time by the endeavor to focus the attention of the student upon the original sources, artistic, scholarly, and documentary. From these, it is hoped, the student may draw not simply some knowledge of human experience but practice in those sensitive, imaginative, and rational skills through which he may inquire into and interpret what men have said and done and what they continue to say and do.

GOVERNMENT AND CONTROL OF THE COLLEGE LIBRARY

EUGENE H. WILSON

GOVERNMENT and control of the college library involve trustees, president, faculty, and librarian, with active control—the carrying-out of policies—usually delegated to the chief librarian. Government and control of the college library have been elements in the internal administration of the liberal arts college in America since 1638. When the Rev. John Harvard in that year, by his will, gave to the college which was to bear his name the sum of £779 17s 2d , in money and some 300 volumes of books, these books probably were the first educational property of a college in this country. In the more than three centuries since that gift, the college in America, the college library, and the government and control of the college library have undergone decided changes. In each of these three areas major changes have occurred in the twentieth century and particularly since the first quarter of this century. In connection with these changes, and probably as a result of them, serious problems appear to exist in the area of government and control of the college library.

My text for this paper is a statement made by Dr. John D. Millett, the executive director of the Commission on Financing Higher Education, in the staff report of the commission which he wrote and which was published less than two years ago. His statement, based on conversations with more than one hundred presidents and deans, is: "Again and again at the institutions we have visited we have found dissatisfaction with and confusion about the library services of higher education."[1] He also wrote in the same report:

Librarians constitutionally hate to throw anything away. They always fear that the book they discard will be the one someone wants next month, and they are always chagrined when they cannot at once produce what is wanted. Moreover, the accrediting associations have tended to "rate" colleges by the number of volumes in the library, regardless of whether anyone uses them or not. Librarians rate the importance of their jobs and examine their salary scale in the light of the size of their book collections, the number of their employees, and their total expenditures. The librarian profession as such puts little emphasis on economy; the pressure comes from college presidents and deans when they make up the annual budget.[2]

Dr. Millett, who was a professor on leave from Columbia University while directing the staff work of the commission, is now a college president. When a librarian wrote and questioned these and other statements in the report, President Millett's reply included the following statements:

I should like to make it clear only that my generalizations about library operations were made on the basis of statements made to me by more than 100 college presidents and deans whom I interviewed throughout the United States. I was endeavoring in my volume simply to report the prevailing consensus of what I was told. . . . Although I didn't say this in my book, I gathered the impression from observations and conversations throughout the United States that where the professional librarian needs to go to work more than any place else is with the ad-

[1] John D. Millett, *Financing Higher Education in the United States* (New York: Columbia University Press, 1952), p. 122.

[2] *Ibid.*, p. 123.

ministrative officials of his own institution. In fact I heard more derogatory language used among the eight presidents who made up the Commission on Financing Higher Education about librarians than I heard about any other component part of university structure. I think this is an unfortunate situation and one which requires attention in the near future.[3]

Let us be among the first to devote attention to this "unfortunate situation." But let us also keep in mind the fact that professors and presidents are not the only critics of the government and control of the library. Three distinguished librarians—Dean Louis R. Wilson, Mildred H. Lowell, and Sarah R. Reed—in the Introduction to *The Library in College Instruction*, which appeared a year *before* Millett's report, wrote that their book was "based upon the conviction held by many college faculties and library staffs that although colleges spend a considerable proportion of their educational budgets for library materials and services, the contribution that the libraries make to furthering the educational program is less than it should be. The libraries fail to convert their full potential educational effectiveness into full educational achievement."[4]

HISTORICAL BACKGROUND

This conference is concerned with the function of the library in the modern college, and the modern college is the college of the twentieth century. A brief consideration of the government and control of colleges and libraries in the seventeenth, eighteenth, and nineteenth centuries will provide essential background.

[3] Association of Research Libraries, "Minutes, January 31, 1954, Madison, Wisconsin," Appendix VI. (Mimeographed.)

[4] Louis R. Wilson, Mildred H. Lowell, and Sarah R. Reed, *The Library in College Instruction* (New York: H. W. Wilson Co., 1951), p. 13.

The General Court of Massachusetts in 1637 ordered a committee composed of the governor, deputy governor, treasurer, three magistrates, and six ministers "to take order for a college at Newetowne." Six years later the court created the Board of Overseers to have full authority over the institution, now named Harvard College. The governor, deputy governor, president of the college, all local magistrates, and the teaching elders of the six adjoining towns composed this board, which in powers and personnel was not greatly different from many modern boards. In 1650 a legally incorporated body to administer the college property was created, and this body, the Harvard Corporation, has continued to this day to provide with the overseers a dual plan of control for Harvard, which has, however, not been adopted by many colleges in the United States. The typical plan of control is a legal body which usually calls itself Trustees, with the president of the college usually an ex officio member. This plan appeared at Yale, Columbia, Princeton, and other early institutions.

In his study of the origins of the American college library, Shores offers the best single source for information on government and control of college libraries in their first stages of development. The early librarians usually had primary responsibilities as teachers, and keeping the library was an added chore. Committees of the faculty or trustees had administrative supervision of the libraries. A faculty committee, with active support of Benjamin Franklin and other trustees, administered the library of the University of Pennsylvania throughout its founding period. "At Pennsylvania, no librarian was appointed until 1855, the faculty assuming the duties ex-officio from 1750 to 1831, and the provost thereafter."[5] Regulations in regard to use of library collections generally were voted by the trustees, and the bylaws of these early boards contain frequent references to various aspects of library administration. Few college librarians in the nineteenth century had a staff of assistants. The librarian at the University of Illinois in 1894 requested that he be replaced by a trained person with trained assistants. The essential points in the history of college libraries before 1900 have been summarized by Lyle as follows:

1. Books were regarded as a necessity in the establishment of colleges and universities.
2. The importance of the library in the educational work of the college was recognized and supported by a considerable number of distinguished presidents in early times.
3. The desirability of special training for the administration and operation of the college library was recognized and the groundwork was laid for professional library education.
4. Certain patterns of procedure in college library administration were definitely established before 1900: the practice of reserving books for large groups of students assigned specific readings; the classification of books based on published classification schemes in place of home-made schedules; the idea of free access to books developed by the student literary society libraries; and the development of technical procedures for the rapid processing and distribution of books.[6]

In a prefatory note to his book *College Administration*, published in 1900, C. F. Thwing, who was then president of Western Reserve University and Adelbert College, stated: "This is, I think, the first book published on the administration of the American college."[7] Twenty-

five years later, Chancellor Capen, of the University of Buffalo, wrote in the Introduction to F. J. Kelly's *The American Arts College:*

Oddly enough, we know very little about the college, in spite of the fact that it is so much discussed. The resources of the new scientific procedures of educational inquiry have seldom been applied to it. Research in college problems has been almost wholly lacking. . . . Educators have long been agreed that essential reorganizations of the system are necessary for the sake both of economy of time and of increased efficiency. That these reorganizations have not taken place has been largely due to the absence of exact information regarding present practices, and the absence of valid definitions of objectives.[8]

President Wilkins of Oberlin College wrote in 1927: "The college, as a living organism, is in constant change. There lie before it, I believe, in the decades soon to come, modifications which will transform it fundamentally. And there are now in process many movements, significant for the future, which have the special interest of contemporaneity.[9]

The literature dealing with the American college, which began to increase significantly in the 1920's, fell into the general categories of surveys of institutions, textbooks and magazine articles of a general nature, reports of foundations and associations, and scientific treatises dealing with limited aspects of the general problems. A similar flowering of literature concerned with the college library began in the 1930's. Dean L. R. Wilson wrote in 1951:

For the past two decades college and university presidents, faculties, library staffs, and edu-

---

[5] Louis Shores, *Origins of the American College Library, 1638–1800* (Nashville: George Peabody College for Teachers, 1934), p. 158.

[6] Guy R. Lyle, *The Administration of the College Library* (2d ed.; New York: H. W. Wilson Co., 1949), p. 5.

[7] Charles F. Thwing, *College Administration* (New York: Century Co., 1900), p. v.

[8] F. J. Kelly, *The American Arts College* (New York: Macmillan Co., 1925), pp. viii–ix.

[9] Ernest H. Wilkins, *The Changing College* (Chicago: University of Chicago Press, 1927), p. 1.

cational foundations and associations have striven to increase the effectiveness of the American college educational program through the improvement of the college library. This effort has been constantly exerted and has expressed itself in many ways.[10]

Dean Wilson then gives several examples to indicate the nature and range of this interest. The Carnegie Corporation of New York, early in the 1930's, made extensive grants-in-aid to more than one hundred junior and liberal arts colleges to strengthen library book collections. Standards of college-library performance were revised by the Southern and the North Central Association of Colleges and Secondary Schools, and lists to be used in checking library resources were published. The first comprehensive study of college libraries made with accurate and inclusive materials appeared in 1932 with the publication of Randall's *The College Library*. In the Introduction to this book, W. W. Bishop wrote:

> The importance of the library in the educational program of the American college is but just coming to be realized. I commend this study of the college libraries to the serious and careful consideration of college trustees and executive officers. The problems considered are real problems which must be met and solved if our college libraries are to function successfully.[11]

The College Library Building by James T. Gerould appeared in 1932, and the Shaw and Mohrhardt lists for college and junior college libraries appeared in 1931 and 1937, respectively. The first book dealing with college-library administration, a collaborative effort by Randall and Goodrich, appeared in 1936. The authors stated in their Introduction:

> Three distinct groups are addressed: (1) the college administrator, who is increasingly concerned with the problems involved in furnishing successful library service to the college, and with the potentialities of the library in an educational program; (2) the college librarian who, it is hoped, may here find material useful in solving the problems of college library administration; and (3) the library-school student, who, as a potential librarian, should be interested in the pages which follow as an introduction to the field of college librarianship.[12]

Lyle in *The Administration of the College Library*, first published in 1944 and in a second edition in 1949; Wilson and Tauber in *The University Library*, published in 1945; and numerous librarians writing in the *Library Quarterly* and in *College and Research Libraries*, which started publication in January, 1931, and in December, 1939, respectively, have covered practically every phase of college-library administration. Special emphasis on the function of the college library in teaching has been dealt with by Wriston in *The Nature of a Liberal College*, Branscomb in *Teaching with Books*, Johnson in *Vitalizing a College Library* and *The Librarian and the Teacher in General Education: A Report of Library-instructional Activities in Stephens College*, and Wilson, Lowell, and Reed in *The Library in College Instruction*, published in 1951, the latest book in this field.

INSTITUTIONAL TYPE AND NATURE OF CONTROL

The institutional type and nature of control of the college as it exists today have significance in our consideration of the library. The term "college" is difficult to define precisely. It is generally accepted as being an institution which admits graduates from standard secondary schools and offers a four-year cur-

[10] Wilson, Lowell, and Reed, *op. cit.*, p. [3].

[11] William M. Randall, *The College Library* (Chicago: American Library Association and the University of Chicago Press, 1932), p. xi.

[12] William M. Randall and Francis L. D. Goodrich, *Principles of College Library Administration* (Chicago: American Library Association and the University of Chicago Press, 1936), p. v.

riculum leading to the Bachelor's degree in arts or science which will qualify the holder for admission to a graduate program in a university or professional school. Various classifications have been made of the types of educational institutions engaged in the formally organized process of higher education.

When the staff of the Commission on Financing Higher Education began its research activities in 1949, the basis for its initial operation was the report of the Exploratory Committee on Financing Higher Education and Research. The exploratory committee had proposed that desirable research studies should be undertaken under two major topics: the nature of American higher education and the financing of higher education. An early step taken by the staff was the development of a new classification scheme for institutions of higher education. This staff technical paper by Richard H. Ostheimer was published in 1951 under the title *A Statistical Analysis of the Organization of Higher Education in the United States, 1948–1949;* the following classification figures are taken from it.

Institutions of higher education were classified into four broad types: universities, separate liberal arts colleges, separate professional schools, and junior colleges. The last three were independent institutions not affiliated with universities. Three basic elements involved in the classification as a university were the offering of an undergraduate liberal arts curriculum, professional education, and graduate study. Liberal arts colleges were divided into two groups of complex (61) and other (392) liberal arts colleges. Professional schools were classed by topic of study. Only accredited institutions were included, except for junior colleges, which were those listed by the United States Office of Education.

The picture by institutional type and nature of control is as follows:

1. Of the 1,532 institutions considered, 36 per cent were under public control and 64 per cent under private control. Of the 121 universities, 53 per cent were public; of 453 liberal arts colleges, 92 per cent were private; of 484 professional schools, 59 per cent were private; and of 474 junior colleges, 52 per cent were public.

2. The 37 public liberal arts colleges included 8 (22 per cent) municipal and 29 (78 per cent) state colleges. The 416 private liberal arts colleges included 65 (16 per cent) nonsectarian, 239 (57 per cent) Protestant, and 112 (27 per cent) Roman Catholic.

3. Average enrolment of the liberal arts colleges was 1,127; average for the public college was 3,249; for the private college, 938.

4. Of the total enrolment in all institutions, 23 per cent was in liberal arts colleges. This 23 per cent of the total enrolment received 41 per cent of the earned degrees in liberal arts, but the universities awarded 51 per cent of the earned degrees in liberal arts.

5. Ninety per cent of earned graduate degrees were awarded by universities, as compared to 6 per cent by liberal arts colleges.

6. Among liberal arts colleges 65 per cent were coeducational, and the percentage of men's and women's colleges was approximately equal. The universities were 98 per cent coeducational.

The typical separate liberal arts college which the college library serves today may be described as a privately controlled, sectarian, coeducational, accredited four-year, degree-conferring institution, with an enrolment of less than 1,000 students. These colleges have 23 per cent of the total enrolment in all institutions of higher education, confer 22 per cent of all earned degrees, 41 per cent of all liberal arts degrees, 13 per cent of professional degrees, and 6 per cent of graduate degrees.

AREAS OF CONCERN

Three major areas of concern in connection with the government and control of the college library are: (1) the legal bases upon which the government of the college rests; (2) the nature of a sound governmental policy for the library; and (3) the relations which the librarian should maintain with the members of the college administrative staff and faculty.

LEGAL BASES OF COLLEGE

The legal bases upon which the government of the college rests follow general patterns, and there have been no significant changes in these patterns in the present century. The privately supported college is established as a legal entity by a charter or articles of incorporation. It is free, within the limits of such documents, to develop its educational policy and program. The Supreme Court of the United States in the Dartmouth College case maintained that Dartmouth's charter was a contract between the state and the college and that the state could not enact legislation which would in effect nullify the charter. As a result of this decision, most states now have laws of incorporation which reserve certain controls, such as the right to alter, amend, or annul charters or articles of incorporation. In recent years the tax-exempt status of private colleges has been receiving increasing attention from legislative bodies.

State or municipal colleges are considered administrative units of government and are subject to the legislature or council of the political unit which created them, unless there is a constitutional provision to the contrary. This legal relation of the college to the city or state may affect the library in such matters as specified routines in the purchase of equipment and supplies, budgetary procedures, and civil service regulations.

CODES OF LIBRARY POLICY OR GOVERNMENT

It is generally agreed by experts in the field of administration that a clearly expressed code of library policy or government is highly desirable, if not essential to efficient library administration. Lyle writes:

It seems self-evident that the college library —involving, as it does, a considerable measure of administrative responsibility, the handling of substantial funds, and relationships with all college officers and faculty—should have a clearly formulated plan of library government to insure its effective operation within the college program. Since the statutes and by-laws in the main fail to clarify this phase of library administration, it might be expected that the library would have a separately published statement of government and control, approved by the faculty and administration and the board of trustees. . . . In the absence of a clearly formulated statement, there is certainly a strong possibility of greater duplication of effort and expense, that cross-purposes will develop, and that the chances for well organized, expertly directed library administration are lessened. The evidence for this is to be found in actual practices in college libraries today.[13]

Wilson and Tauber write:

The nature of the policy which governs the internal organization and administration of the university library depends, in most cases, on the prescribed regulations, by-laws, and proceedings of the governing body of the university or of the faculty or senate or other university body to which the governing body has delegated authority for formulating such policy. This is true of both public and private institutions. However, in a number of instances universities have not formulated such policies; or the formal regulations and by-laws which they have adopted for

[13] Lyle, *op. cit.*, pp. 39–40.

the government of their libraries fail to include such important matters as the scope and objectives of the library, the functions and responsibilities of the librarian and members of the staff, and the organic relationships of the library to other units and officials of the institution. In recent surveys of university libraries it has been found that lack of clarity on such points as these is usually attended by a corresponding lack of efficiency and adequacy of library services.[14]

A consensus of students of this problem indicates that a code of library policy or government should include the following points:

I. A clear definition of the physical aspects of the library.
   A. What college-purchased materials belong to the library.
   B. Whether or not there are departmental libraries, and if so where located and whether under department or library control.
II. An unequivocal statement in regard to personnel.
   A. Status and tenure of the director and the library staff, both professional and clerical.
   B. The relation of the librarian to the controlling body of the college and the officer to whom he is directly responsible.
   C. The librarian's major duties in library administration, and where his authority begins and ends.
   D. Any additional duties commonly assigned to him.
   E. Right of participation of the whole library personnel in group benefit plan.
III. Objectives of the library in relation to those of the college.
   A. As an instructional unit.
   B. As an aid to research.
   C. Additional services to students, faculty and the community.
IV. A statement concerning library finances.
   A. Who makes decisions on budget requirements for purchases of materials for library purposes, and for purchase of library equipment.
   B. What role the library committee plays in budget planning.
V. A statement on the library committee.
   A. How it is chosen.

[14] Wilson and Tauber, *op. cit.*, p. 24.

B. Its composition.
C. Term of office of its members.
D. Its principal functions, and what absolute powers it may exercise, if any.[15]

A recent study by Biggs to determine present college practices in regard to codes of library government indicates that "few college libraries have such rules in addition to their charter and bylaws."[16] A questionnaire was sent by Miss Biggs to 214 accredited, coeducational, privately controlled, four-year, degree-granting institutions in the United States, and 111 questionnaires were filled out completely enough to be usable for the study. Questions were divided into six groups: (1) the college government and the library, (2) the physical library, its contents and divisions, (3) personnel, (4) administration, including financing and the library's objectives, (5) the library committee, (6) codes for library government. Types of legal instruments authorizing the institutions were reported as charters in 46 institutions, articles of incorporation in 22, charter and articles of incorporation in 39, other in 1. Types of rules of the governing body of the institutions were reported as bylaws in 84 institutions, statutes in 3, bylaws and statutes in 8, and other in 4. Only 5 of the legal instruments authorizing the colleges mentioned the library. One authorizes library purchases, 2 include the librarian with the faculty, 1 gives as a purpose of the college "to provide libraries," and 1 lists the librarian's duties and responsibilities. Bylaws, statutes, or other rules of the governing bodies of 16 institutions mention the library or librarian briefly (the librarian usually in connection with his status as a member of the faculty),

[15] Martha Biggs, *Codifying College Library Policy* ("University of Illinois Library School Occasional Papers," No. 14 [1950]), p. 11.
[16] *Ibid.*, p. 1.

the requirement of an annual report to the trustees, formation of a library committee, or duties and qualifications of the librarians. Fifty-one librarians reported no official statement of what constitutes library materials, 36 did not answer the question, and 24 named various places where such statements might be found. College catalogs offer a certain amount of accounting of library holdings. Staff handbooks, codes, and statements of working policies sometimes include such information.

A statement of library objectives was reported in existence in only 31 colleges. In 14 cases the statement was in the college catalog; in 10 no location was mentioned; in 3 it was in a statement of working policy; in 2 it was in a library committee report; in 1 in the annual report of the librarian; and in 1 in the faculty handbook. Statements of objectives examined by Miss Biggs were expressed in general terms of teaching students how to use library materials, encouraging good reading and study habits, broadening reading interests, and providing curricular and research materials.

In replying to the question as to whether a need was felt for a clearly expressed and definite code of library policy, 16 reported such a code in use, 26 indicated its need, 32 stated no such additional code was desirable, and 35 did not answer the question. Several answers stated that fine library-faculty administrative relations eliminated the need for such a statement. A small group said that the fewer the rules for the library, the better.

Since a minority of the 111 librarians reported a code or indicated they felt the need of such codification of library policy, it appears that there is no definite trend toward written codes, despite the recommendations of writers in the field of library administration. Changes which occur in the position of college president and college librarian are relatively frequent when compared to major changes in the government and control of the library and would appear to be a particularly strong reason why a written code should replace unwritten agreements or policy.

THE LIBRARIAN'S RELATIONS TO COMPONENTS OF THE COLLEGE

The librarian, as the chief officer of an agency serving the entire college, may have relations with all members of the college. In the case of the university librarian, Wilson and Tauber list 33 various university and nonuniversity groups, agencies, and individuals with which the librarian and his staff may have administrative, business, instruction, service, or research relations. Since the typical college is considerably smaller and less complex than the typical university, a similar list for the college would be only about half as long as the university list and would ordinarily include the following: trustees, president, legislative faculty, library committee, deans, heads of departments, faculty members, college committees, other libraries in the community, union catalogs and bibliographical centers, students, business office, buildings and grounds, general public, faculty families, employees of the college, alumni, friends' groups. These relations have been discussed in detail in library literature, and the principles involved are familiar to the college librarian who attempts to keep abreast of developments in this field.

However, two areas in this field of government and control of the college library, those involving library relations with administrative officers and relations with faculty, appear to deserve special consideration at this time. The more serious problem appears to be in regard to the relationships that prevail with administrative officers, assuming that Millett's statements have a basis in fact.

Numerous statements by college presidents to the effect that the library is the heart of the college may be cited. In the same year that Millett's report was published, Raymond M. Hughes, with long experience as a professor, college president, and college trustee, wrote in a book on problems of college and university administration:

The importance of a library to a college becomes apparent as one studies the need it fills. Having taught chemistry in a college prior to becoming its president, I took a number of years to realize that the library should be generously supported. It was difficult for me to believe that more money should be spent for the staff than for the books, journals and bindings in a library. It was hard to understand that inevitably a considerable portion of books bought would be used very little, if at all. I did not know that next to the college faculty itself, the library was the most important adjunct of a college. However, I did finally learn the prime value of a college or university library.[17]

This book devotes 10 pages to the library, considerably more attention than is usually given in such books. A study of the treatment of the college library in general books published since 1900 on college administration, submitted to the School of Library Science at Western Reserve University in 1949, reported that "of 53 titles examined, 23 contained information about the library."[18] In the majority of these books the information was in the form of scattered references rather than a unified treatment. The author does note that over the years changes occurred in the topics discussed. Thwing in 1900 in his chapter on "Financial Relations" devoted four pages to the library as a special object in a college to which a donor should give. While the earlier books usually dealt in such generalities, more recent books considered specific problems, such as business aspects of operating a college library, budget and library costs, new library services, teaching function of the college library, and professional status of the college librarian.

The principles of relationships of the college library to administrative officers, faculty, and students have been stated frequently and are generally accepted. Within the last five years several attempts have been made to determine the extent to which these principles are actually followed in college-library administration. The questionnaire method was employed by Kientzle in a study of the relationships among college and university administrators, library committees, and librarians; by Peeler in a study of the functions and duties of faculty library committees in colleges; by Gelfand in a study of the college librarian in the academic community; and by Wilson, Lowell, and Reed in a study of the library in college instruction.[19]

The President and the Librarian.— Generally accepted principles governing the relation of the president to the librarian are: (1) the librarian should be appointed by and should be directly responsible to the president; and (2) the

[17] Frank L. McVey and Raymond M. Hughes, *Problems of College and University Administration* (Ames: Iowa State College Press, 1952), p. 293.

[18] Harriet A. Wise, "A Study of the Treatment of the College Library in General Books on College Administration" (M.S. report, School of Library Science, Western Reserve University, 1949), p. 3.

[19] Elizabeth F. Kientzle, "The College Librarian and the Library Committee," *Library Quarterly*, XXI (1951), 120–26; Elizabeth Peeler, "Functions and Duties of Faculty Library Committees in Colleges" (unpublished Master's thesis, School of Library Service, Columbia University, 1950); Morris A. Gelfand, "The College Librarian in the Academic Community," *College and Research Libraries*, X (1949), 129–34, 139; Wilson, Lowell, and Reed, *op. cit.*

librarian should have a close and significant relationship to the educational program. This second principle may be achieved if the president places the librarian on policy-making committees or develops through conferences with him the policies for integrating the library with the educational program.

Kientzle in a study of 89 midwestern colleges found that more than three-fourths of the librarians had been appointed by and were responsible to the president. In 20 institutions, mainly the larger ones, the librarian reported to some officer other than the president. Only 12 per cent of the librarians held regularly scheduled conferences with the president. Many librarians complained about the infrequency of meetings with the president, apparently having a conference only when required by an acute problem. Few librarians indicated that too limited access to the president resulted in definitely unsatisfactory relations with the administration; but 18 felt that steps might be taken to improve the situation; and some reported their opinion that the administration gave too little attention to the library. Several indicated the need of a definite code of library policy in regard to library-administration-faculty relationships, but a considerable number indicated they preferred a minimum of attention on the part of the administration to library operations.

In the larger institutions more frequently than in the smaller the librarian held membership on policy-making committees. A slight majority, 53 per cent, of the librarians in all the institutions studied by Kientzle belonged to at least one such committee. Gelfand reported that relatively few chief librarians served on important college committees and that library staff members rarely serve on any college committee of importance.

The President and the Library Committee.—Peeler's study was an attempt "to determine specifically the functions of existing faculty library committees; to ascertain in each case in what manner the actual committees act in fulfilling these duties; and to present authoritative opinion on the advisability of this committee action."[20] Questionnaires were sent to a selected list of 125 college libraries east of the Rockies. Eleven reported no library committees, and 72 returned the questionnaires with sufficient information to make them the basis of this study. Twenty-two functions of library committees were identified and used as the basis of the questionnaire. Eight author-administrator experts in the college-library field participated in presenting the authoritative opinion.

The principles of appointment, structure, and form of organization of the library committee have been summarized as follows:

1. The committee should be appointed on the recommendation of the librarian and by the officer to whom the librarian is responsible.

2. It should be representative of the interests of the college as a whole, rather than of the departments individually.

3. It should be made up chiefly of faculty members, although the librarian and the president or his representative should also be included.

4. The chairman should be a teaching member of the faculty, with recognized qualities of leadership.

5. The number of members recommended varies from four to ten.

6. Membership should be rotated, and terms of office should overlap.

7. Minutes of meetings should be distributed to the faculty as well as the committee.[21]

[20] Peeler, *op. cit.*, p. 8.

[21] Kientzle, *op. cit.*, pp. 121–22.

The extent to which these principles are reflected in practice as reported by Kientzle, Peeler, and Gelfand follows:

1. Presidents appointed two-thirds of the committees in each group. Peeler reported 7 committees elected by direct faculty vote, 6 by indirect faculty action, 2 were composed completely of ex officio members (heads of departments), and 1 was elected by trustees. Kientzle found that less than half were appointed with the advice of the librarian; Peeler found the librarian was not consulted in 19 colleges, had the right to recommend faculty members in 19 colleges, and in 3 colleges the names were submitted to the librarian by the president for approval.

2. Peeler found that appointments on the basis of departmental or divisional representation were almost twice as common as appointments based on personal qualifications of individual faculty members or appointments based on a combination of both. One librarian reported "No basis," another, "Neither, in my judgment."

3. The librarian was a member of the committee in each of Peeler's 72 colleges, and in 90 per cent of the colleges studied by Gelfand. Presidents or deans are included as members in less than half of the colleges, and rarely attend meetings.

4. The president appointed the chairman in more than half the Peeler group, in more than one-third of the Kientzle group. The librarian served as ex officio chairman or secretary or both in two-fifths of the Peeler group and in one-third of the Kientzle group.

5. Peeler reported the number of committee members ranged from 3 to 18, with a mode of 5, and only two committees had student members. Kientzle reported a range of from 5 to 9 members.

6. Appointments generally were for an indefinite period, or for one year with reappointments being customary.

7. Meetings generally are not held on a regular schedule. Peeler found 16 colleges with definite schedules for meetings and 52 on irregular or indefinite schedule. A number of committees report no minutes are kept and, where kept, are usually not distributed or are distributed to committee members only.

These findings support the conclusions that the college administration has little concern with the organization of the library committee, presidents rarely attend their meetings, the faculty know little of their work, and there is not general application of accepted principles of college-library committee organization in practices reported by more than one hundred colleges.

The Librarian and the Library Committee.—Neither Peeler nor Kientzle reports a library committee with full powers of government. Each found that 90 per cent of the committees were wholly advisory, and 10 per cent had limited administrative powers, mainly in connection with matters of finance. A comparison of opinions of the experts who cooperated in the Peeler study with actual practice in 72 libraries in connection with 22 functions of existing library committees results in some interesting findings.

In summary, expert opinion agreed with prevailing practice on ten functions, disagreed on nine, and was divided on three. In the area of agreement, five of the functions were ones which the experts did not approve and which were not followed by a majority of committees: establishing salary schedules, supervising special phases of library service, requiring a continuing statement on the balance of the budget, approving all titles purchased, exerting a right of censorship. Functions which expert opinion approved and on which practice agreed were: determining rules of library service, controlling special grants, supplying services of subject specialists in acquisition, acting on faculty requests, and approving library building plans. In most of these functions agreement in practice usually was by a slight majority. Functions on which expert opinion was divided were: establishing general policies of service, requiring a report from the librarian to the committee, reporting from the committee to the faculty. The nine functions on which prevailing practice did not follow the opinions of the experts deserve our consideration as possible clues to some of the reasons for "dissatisfaction with and confusion about the library services of higher education."

The experts were unanimous in thinking the library committee should act in an advisory capacity in selection of the librarian and of the staff; yet 82 per cent of the committees did not act in this capacity. While the problem of selecting a librarian may occur infrequently, selection of staff members may occur with sufficient frequency to provide, in the carrying-out of this function by the committee, an opportunity for better understanding between the library, the faculty, and the administration.

Expert opinion was unanimous in favoring advisory action by the committee in establishing the amount of the budget request; yet only 47 per cent of the committees so acted. Kientzle found that no more than 37 per cent of the committees gave consideration to the library budget and that only rarely did such consideration result in suggestions for changes. The advisory function of allocating the budget to departments was favored by the experts; yet only 36 per cent gave such advice, 38 per cent took no action, and 26 per cent apportioned funds. Kientzle found 16 per cent of the committees apportioned book funds, while 84 per cent took no part in allocating or merely adopted the suggestions

of the librarian. The experts favored advisory action in the approval of large purchases or expensive titles; but only 10 per cent of the committees reviewed such purchases, and 30 per cent offered advisory action. Kientzle reported 17 per cent of committees reviewed such expensive purchases.

Fifty-eight per cent of the committees took no action in establishing or maintaining a systematic plan for building the book collection, although there was unanimous expert opinion that this should be an advisory function. Such a plan, developed and supported by a faculty committee, can be a most effective means of justifying budget requests to the president, who must be concerned with total college expenditures, and certainly is closely related to the educational program of the college. The experts believe that the library committee should act in an advisory capacity in regard to questionable titles, although a majority of the committees do not so act. The experts favor a regular reporting from the committee to the administration; but the majority of committees make no report at all.

There is unanimous opinion among the experts in favoring advisory assistance by the committees in interpreting the library to the faculty and in the promotion of public relations for the library. The majority of the committees do not provide such advisory assistance, and 61 per cent of the committees are reported as taking no action in promoting public relations for the libraries. The importance of such action is emphasized in a survey article on public relations for college and university libraries by Robert W. Orr which appeared in the first issue of *Library Trends*.[22]

[22] Robert W. Orr, "Public Relations for College and University Libraries," *Library Trends*, I (1952), 123–35.

On the basis of expert opinion of the functions which should be served by college-library committees acting in an advisory capacity, it is apparent that the committees fall far short of making their full contribution. Some committees are effective, but it is clear that most committees are not nearly so effective as they would be if librarians and presidents utilized these groups to fulfil the functions agreed upon by the experts as being proper and desirable.

What is the opinion of the librarians in regard to their committees? In response to a question asked in the Kientzle investigation, 64 per cent of the librarians answered unequivocally that their working relationship with their library committee was satisfactory, 30 per cent indicated satisfaction with their committees but admitted the possibility of improving the working relationship, and only 6 per cent were dissatisfied because of too much action or interference in administrative affairs by their committees. It should be noted that some librarians stated their satisfaction was due to the dormant condition of their committee. The librarians were also asked whether they considered their committee performed a very useful function, was moderately useful, or served almost no useful function. Forty-five per cent regarded their committee as very useful, and 41 per cent moderately useful. Librarians of colleges which had no library committees, generally in smaller institutions, reported direct and cordial relations with faculty and administration which appeared to approach the ideal.

THE LIBRARIAN IN THE HIERARCHY OF THE COLLEGE

Where does the librarian stand in the hierarchy of the college? President Hughes writes:

Quite the most important thing about a library is the librarian. If he is of first class caliber, the money appropriated for the library will be well spent; the service to patrons will be good and every department will have, within the limits of its resources, all the books and journals it needs. Certainly, a salary as large as any dean in the college receives, is due a high-grade librarian.[23]

One concrete demonstration of where the librarian stands in the college organization is provided by comparing the salary he receives with salaries received by administrative personnel and by the faculty in the colleges. Such figures are available in a research study published recently by the National Education Association and covering salaries paid in 1952–53.[24] Tabulation of salaries paid administrative personnel in 80 non-publicly supported colleges with enrolments of fewer than 500 students reveals that the median salaries for 12 months received by ten of the administrative officers most often found in colleges (deans of administration, students, men, and women, director of admissions, registrar, business manager, director of publicity, director of athletics, and librarian) range from $3,350 to $5,325. The median salary of librarians is $3,600, ranking in eighth position, ahead of the registrar at $3,350 and the dean of women at $3,400. Salaries paid on a 9-month basis to the teaching staff in this same group of colleges in 1952–53 reveal a median of $3,350 for top salaries to instructors, $3,600 to assistant professors, $3,967 to associate professors, and $4,350 to professors. The median salary of $3,600 for 12-month service as librarian is less than the top salary an instructor would receive for the same period.

Tabulation of salaries paid admin-

[23] McVey and Hughes, *op. cit.*, p. 295.

[24] "Salary-Schedule Provisions or Salaries Paid in Degree-granting Institutions, 1952–1953," *NEA Research Bulletin*, XXXI (December, 1953), 160–66.

istrative personnel in 61 nonpublicly supported colleges with enrolments of 500–999 students reveals that the median salaries for 12 months received by the same ten officers range from $4,000 to $6,000. The median salary of librarians is $4,000, which ties with the median salary of registrars for last place among the ten administrative officers. Salaries paid on a 9-month basis to the teaching staff in this same group of colleges in 1952–53 reveal a median of $3,575 for top salaries to instructors, $4,000 to assistant professors, $4,500 to associate professors, and $4,950 to professors. The median salary of $4,000 for 12 months' service as librarian is approximately what the top salary of an instructor would be for the same period.

Tabulation of salaries paid administrative personnel in 31 nonpublicly supported colleges with enrolments of 1,000 or more students reveals approximately the same comparative position of the librarian's salary. The median salaries for 12 months received by the same ten administrative officers range from $4,500 to $7,600. The median salary of the librarians in this group of colleges is $5,010, ranking in eighth position ahead of the director of publicity at $4,500 and the dean of women at $4,900. Salaries paid on a 9-month basis in 1952–53 to the teaching staff in this group of colleges reveal a median of $4,150 for top salaries to instructors, $4,650 to assistant professors, $5,300 to associate professors, and $6,050 to professors. The median salary of $5,010 for 12 months' service as librarian is approximately what the top salary of an instructor would be for the same period.

These figures of salaries actually paid in 1952–53 indicate that the librarian, at least in terms of salary, ranks well toward the bottom of the administrative group, and only at the top of the instruc-tor's rank in the academic group. Although the librarians of most colleges have achieved the green pastures of professorial rank, it appears evident that their salaries do not correspond to those of their colleagues of the classroom teaching staff. Kientzle reported that in the colleges which were included in her study, approximately half the librarians held the Master's degree and 24 per cent the doctorate. This would indicate that the head librarian in the college ordinarily has academic and professional qualifications equivalent to those of the group of instructors in the academic faculty or of lower-ranking administrative officers.

The relationship of the librarian to the classroom teacher and to students in a direct connection with the educational program of the college has implications for the government and control of the library. The Introduction to the Wilson, Lowell, and Reed book on *The Library in College Instruction* informs us that, "while it is designed to give instructors some appreciation of the problems of library administration and to make them better collaborators with college librarians and library committees, it is especially intended to unite instructor and librarian in an understanding of library problems and methods."[25] Since the contents of this book should be familiar to college librarians, a mere reference to it should be sufficient in this connection.

SUMMARY AND CONCLUSION

Various aspects of the government and control of the college library have been considered in relation to statements that dissatisfaction with and confusion about the library services of higher education exist, that relations between the librarian and the administrative officers of his institution require attention, and that college libraries are

[25] Wilson, Lowell, and Reed, *op. cit.*, p. 14.

failing to convert their potential educational effectiveness into full educational achievement.

The increasing attention being devoted to the college and to the college library during the last twenty-five years, as evidenced by the growing body of literature, has been pointed out. The principles which are basic to the solution of problems in the area have been formulated and generally accepted. Why do the problems appear to continue unsolved? The answers to this question may lie in the following conclusions:

1. College librarians generally do not operate under clearly expressed codes of library policy or government for their specific institutions.

2. College librarians do not have regular conferences with, or frequent access to, their presidents.

3. College librarians generally are not members of policy-making committees.

4. Accepted principles of college-library committee organization are not generally applied in practices reported by colleges.

5. Library committees are not nearly so effective as they would be if librarians and presidents utilized these groups to fulfil the functions agreed upon by experts as being proper and desirable.

6. College librarians, at least in terms of salary received, rank well toward the bottom of the administrative group, and only at the top of the instructor's rank in the academic group.

Does the fault lie in our administrative superiors, or in our faculty colleagues, or "in ourselves, that we are underlings"? Gaining academic rank, gaining admission to membership in the American Association of University Professors, gaining the president's ear, being appointed to policy-making committees, even moving up in the college salary brackets—all these achievements are desirable but will not of themselves remove dissatisfaction with library services, create ideal relations with administrative officers and teachers, and result in full educational achievement by the library.

These problems in the area of government and control of the college library will be solved, or reduced to manageable proportions, only when college librarians achieve the following: (1) a clearly expressed and established code of library policy; (2) an advisory library committee functioning with maximum effectiveness; (3) a clear distinction between clerical and professional duties, and the separation of these duties so that professional members of the staff are free from clerical duties; (4) a positive role in contributing to the college's educational program by making the library a real teaching agency; (5) a record of research or professional accomplishments comparable to those of faculty members; and (6) academic and professional qualifications equivalent to those of top administrative or teaching colleagues.

Responsibility for achieving these points does not rest solely with librarians. College libraries will convert their full potential educational effectiveness into full educational achievement only when presidents, faculties, and librarians share fully and equally in this responsibility.

THE LIBERAL ARTS FUNCTION OF THE UNIVERSITY LIBRARY

STANLEY E. GWYNN

THE inclusion of an article on the university library in a series of papers devoted to the college library has baffled a number of the laity and may possibly have raised a professional eyebrow or two. It will be well, accordingly, to remind, not this audience, but the wider and more general audience that will read these published papers, that a large number of colleges are attached to universities and that most such colleges are served by university libraries. There are differences, however, between college and university libraries, and certain characteristics of the large university library make it reasonable to wonder whether such an institution can function as well, in relation to the undergraduate user, as does the smaller college library. For these reasons, no consideration of the library in the modern college would be complete without some examination of the way in which these larger libraries serve, or should serve, their undergraduate clientele.

But, although the topic may be appropriate for this conference, one may still question the need to discuss this matter. To many librarians, perhaps to many of you, the question must seem already to have been settled. The differences between the typical college library and the large university library have been obvious for a long time, and many university librarians have decided that they do make the university library unsuitable for college students. Accordingly, some librarians have altered their physical plants, redistributed their collections, and modified their services in the hope that their institutions would thereby be made more appropriate for undergraduate use. Moreover, the negative answer may have been the correct answer, and the suggested solutions the correct solutions, for professional library literature contains numerous reports which assert that these efforts apparently are realizing the hopes held out for them. What room, then, for a discussion such as this if the hypotheses have been acted upon, tested, and found valid?

There are several reasons which justify exploring this subject. One, of course, is that many university librarians still face this problem and still have a decision to make. Another is that some of the solutions thus far offered and put into effect have taken the shape of small college libraries within the university library system. The implicit assumption is that the typical college-library pattern is a valid pattern—and that assumption needs analysis. Again, even a casual knowledge of some undergraduate library programs suggests that these libraries are undertaking activities that perhaps are not very closely related to the logical functions of the undergraduate library. These need to be looked at with some suspicion, since so many experiments in librarianship have left their bleached bones on the desert called "teaching with books." Another reason lies in the fact that, despite the increased recognition of the library on the college scene and despite much lip service to the ideal of teaching with books and to the value of doing what is called "integrating the library with the teaching program," librarians are inclined to feel that little, if any, real integration has occurred at either the college or the university level. This failure may be related to our present problem, and we may properly wonder whether we have tried to integrate the wrong things, or the right things in the wrong ways. Finally, there is this reason for this discussion: any profession should continually re-examine its activities—even, or perhaps especially, those that seem the most promising or successful. We have, then, a problem which should interest all librarians serving undergraduates, and a problem which we may tentatively assume has not yet been solved to the general satisfaction.

I have remarked that the differences which distinguish the university from the college library are obvious. To list them at this point will be the easiest way into this discussion. The first difference is the sheer bulk of the book collection. The university library may just simply contain too many physical volumes for the undergraduate student, and, as a result, he may be confused and thwarted in his attempts to find anything at all, much less the right book for his purpose. The second university library characteristic lies in the nature of the book collection itself. It is a research collection, and as such it contains a far greater variety of books on every subject than does the college library. Some of these are by competent authors, and some are not. Some are broad treatments of a subject, and some are intensive studies of but a minute aspect of a field of knowledge. Some are definitive statements, while others have already been superseded by a dozen other titles—which also are in the library. A great many materials are not literary, historical, critical, or synthesizing in any way but have been

gathered as the raw materials for future research, their very *raison d'être* in the collection baffling except to the scholar or librarian. Third, the catalog which provides the key to these huge and varied collections is necessarily so large and so complex that it is likely to prove altogether mysterious to the college student. Fourth, the reference staff, which ordinarily might be expected to help the undergraduate overcome some of the difficulties already named, may be so occupied in meeting the demands of the graduate students and faculty that undergraduate needs either are ignored or are given cursory attention. Too, the kind of staff assembled for research library purposes is not necessarily the kind of staff that can work most effectively with younger students. Finally, considerations of size usually make it expedient for the university library to close its stacks to undergraduates, thus depriving them of free access to books. Similar considerations frequently lead to the establishment of reserve-book rooms and other devices that may not be educationally satisfactory. And, over all, there is the large building or series of buildings necessary to house all these books and catalogs and service activities, and this, because of size, is likely to be impersonal and frustrating for the uninitiated.

These are the essential differences, and these are the characteristics that lead the librarian to ask: Can the undergraduate student effectively use this large collection, this variety of books, this perplexing catalog, and this frequently too impersonal complex of services we have provided?

If the question is put this way, the answer in most cases must be, "No, he cannot." Should the librarian therefore provide a smaller collection specifically for the undergraduate, in which will be placed those books he is most likely to use? Should he provide a special staff and a special catalog? Before he makes such decisions, or others less drastic, it may be that he should first recognize that the characteristics of the university library have positive as well as negative values for the undergraduate users of its collections and services. The book collections have all the kinds of books a college library has, and in greater abundance and variety. The service staff includes a number of subject specialists who, taken together, will have both a broader range and a greater depth of bibliographical knowledge than the relatively small staff of the college library. There may be virtue even in the large catalog. Perhaps, instead of separating both research books and research staff from the college student, they should be brought together.

The possibilities inherent in this alternative view will become clearer if we look at the questions our librarian has been asking. All of them have been asked in relation to the capacities or abilities of the student—not in relation to his educational needs. I deduce from the literature that this is the way librarians have most often asked their questions. Or they have asked, in effect, "is the library simple enough for the students to be able to use it?"—which is another way of saying, "Are the students knowledgeable enough to use the library we have provided for them?"

I suggest that perhaps the wrong questions have been asked and that they have been asked in relation to the wrong things. I suggest that the university librarian must ask, not *can* the student use our library facilities, but *should* the undergraduate students be able to use our library? And he must also ask whether the library is adequate for the *needs* of the students, meaning, when he asks, their absolute educational needs, not what the students themselves think their needs are and not even what the faculty or the college president think the library needs are.

If the questions are asked in this way, I think that the answer to both must be Yes. The student, of course, is temporarily left in the same uncomfortable position—he has difficulty using the university library. But if this is the correct approach to the problem, then the university librarian will be less concerned with changing his library to match the undergraduate capacities and will devote himself rather to attempts to bring the students' abilities up to the level of the library and its services. I would not be misunderstood. There probably are concessions to undergraduate use that are necessary or desirable in every university library. Our chief concern should be, however, that the concessions be made with the proper ends in mind—and the proper ends are the educational needs of the student.

What are these needs? What are the liberal arts, and what are the instruments used by the liberal arts college to train the student in them? A few decades ago the phrase "liberal arts" would not have needed definition. Recently, however, the widespread probings into the aims and methods of higher education have rung so many changes on the term that one cannot use it with any assurance that one will be understood. These newer educational concepts range all the way from what is described quite simply as "general education" to something which has been set forth in a book bearing the alarming title *A College Curriculum Based on Functional Needs of Students*. In view of these circumstances, I fear that the definition I am about to offer will fall quaintly on the ear. I feel, however, that it embraces all the valid conceptions, both old and new.

The liberal arts, then, by a still useful definition of the Romans, are those arts which a free man ought to be versed in; and, to add a more modern and somewhat expanded concept, they are also, by a happy reciprocal action, those very arts which *make* men free.

What the specific arts are, within this framework, and what subjects contribute to their mastery are matters open to continuing discussion. I will assert, however, that there is in our society general agreement as to what constitutes a liberal education, and general acceptance of the fact that the four-year liberal arts college is the agency that best imparts that education. It is possible to say, therefore, that the aim and office of the so-called "liberal arts college" is, first, to give the secondary-school graduate a broader and deeper knowledge and appreciation of man's history, of his cultural achievements, and of the bases for his conduct, to the end that he may take his place as a basically informed member of a democratic society; second, to teach him those intellectual attitudes and skills that will enable him to become, through his own continuing self-education after the A.B., an increasingly informed, intelligent, and dynamic force in that society; and, third, to give him what amounts to an incidental by-product but what is the most valuable of all —a sense of values.

If we are agreed that these are the aims of the liberal arts college, I hope we will also agree that the college's primary instruments toward achieving those ends are the course of study and the faculty. The library is auxiliary to these instruments, and its task is to implement the design of the program and the work of the instructional staff.

I do not need to rehearse in detail the ways in which the college library performs these auxiliary services. They are well known to all of you. I will just say briefly, therefore, that the library's functions are to provide the books that the faculty and students require for formal instruction, to provide additional collections of the classic and other important works in all areas of knowledge, to supply as many as possible of the materials needed for faculty research, and to maintain a good collection of reference works and bibliographical apparatus. All these must, of course, be made available under comfortable and convenient physical conditions, and there must be a competent staff to assist the readers in their use of the library and to relate the library to the aims of the college.

For many of these requirements the university library, as we have already seen, is more adequate than the college library. The embarrassments are that students generally make less use of these collections than we think they should (in either the college or the university library), and that only a few students know how to use the library. Moreover, we will admit, if we are honest, that these statements are as true of most of the libraries that have created special programs and facilities as they are of those libraries that have made no special effort.

How serious is this lack of use and lack of knowledge in relation to the purposes of the college? If we look again at the aims of the liberal arts college as I defined them above, we will, I think, grant that the student will get, from the faculty and through his courses, the first kind of education; that is, his knowledge of man's history, cultural achievements, and the bases for man's conduct. Some of this will have come to him through his use of the library in response to assigned readings or specific suggestions from his instructors. Only a handful of students will have used the library independently, but an education will have been acquired nevertheless. Look again at the second purpose of the liberal arts college: to teach the student those intellectual attitudes and skills which will enable him to become, through his own continuing self-education after the A.B., an increasingly informed, intelligent, and dynamic force in his society. Here, too, we must grant that most of these attitudes and skills are inculcated or taught by the faculty. Indeed, it is only rarely that attitudes come initially from books, though they may be fortified by them, and most skills must be taught. Obviously, however, there is one skill that has not been taught at all or has been taught inadequately. Yet it is an important skill if the student is to get a better education while in college and if he is to continue his self-education after his college days. That skill, of course, is skill in the use of books and libraries.

When I say that these matters have not been taught at all, I am not, of course, unaware of the widespread use of orientation courses taught by librarians or the units on the library wedged into the opening weeks of the English course and taught by the faculty. I have heard, too, that in a few colleges every assignment made by instructors is calculated to advance the student's knowledge of the use of books and libraries. But all these methods, even the most constructive one mentioned last, are too narrowly conceived and executed. What is needed is something both broader and more basic.

One of the most important require-ments is that the student be given an understanding of the library as a social agency. Man owes his achievements to the fact that he has found ways to record and preserve his experiences so that other men might learn from them and build beyond them. Ever since the invention of printing and the spread of literacy, the records of man's knowledge and speculations have grown and continue to grow at what appear to be exponential rates. These records constitute, in a quite literal sense, the memory of civilization. In society it is the office of the librarian to assume an active custodianship of that memory. By "active" I mean to imply, among other things, the operation of the selective and organizing function, without which memory, whether in the individual brain or in the form of millions of books, is a mass of unusable facts. Society relies on the librarian and other indexers and bibliographers to maintain the best possible bibliographical control over the twenty-five million separate works of knowledge that have appeared, and the additional millions of separate editions. The individual librarian's first task is to select from the vast universe of print those relatively few items likely to be needed by the agency or social group which retains his services. And his second task is to arrange and index his own collection so that the needed materials can be found if he has them.

I have taken a few moments thus to describe what you already know because I think that all this represents a really quite dramatic activity whose drama has never been fully appreciated outside the profession and is frequently lost on librarians themselves. It is more than dramatic, however; it is a major function in society and a function steadily increasing in importance. Finally, it is intimately related to the work that goes on in the college and university and is one of the indispensable props of education.

Since it is all this, a knowledge of the purpose of libraries, the role of librarians, and the methods by which they control and make available this memory of civilization seems to me to be not only a proper but a necessary element of the liberal arts curriculum. Further, the skill required to use a library—that enables the student to select, from that portion of society's memory which is represented by his college or university library collection, those materials pertinent to his problems—seems to be one of the skills which the college exists to provide. Indeed, I will boldly assert that in these times and in our present state of learning, with the records of knowledge multiplying at an almost uncontrollable rate (bibliographically speaking), *the knowledge and skills we have been talking about actually constitute one of the liberal arts.*

If this is not entirely fanciful on my part, what should be taught, when, and by whom? The details of the program require a careful consideration, for which there is neither time nor space in this paper, but the following knowledge and skills would appear to be the minimum requirements:

1. A fundamental knowledge of the role of the library and the librarian in society
2. A general understanding of the means by which recorded knowledge is kept track of—listed, indexed, abstracted, and made available through various kinds of catalogs, subject bibliographies, etc.
3. A theoretical knowledge of the ways in which libraries are arranged, and why, with special, practical emphasis on the student's own library
4. A thorough, practical knowledge of the workings of the card catalog, and particularly of the subject approach (by this I mean mastery not of a simplified catalog but of the most complex catalog the school's library affords)
5. A knowledge of the common kinds of reference tools and of specific titles among them, with an eventual knowledge of the more specialized guides, handbooks, and bibliographies

When this instruction should be given is also a matter for careful thought. The answer will vary from school to school, but ideally it would seem that the matters dealing with the characteristics and use of printed guides should be made an integral part of many of the courses the student will take throughout his college career. The material under the first four headings should come fairly early, but not before the student's course work requires regular use of the library. Who should offer this instruction is clear. The faculty should. But the majority of faculty members lack the requisite knowledge, and the problem of educating them presents difficulties that will take a long time to solve. The best hope and the greatest desideratum is a really good syllabus designed especially with these purposes, this audience, and this teaching staff in mind. Initially, however, the librarian will have to accept the teaching responsibility.

I would like to repeat that the instruction I have outlined differs from present courses primarily in emphasis and thoroughness. Library instruction now generally ignores and certainly minimizes the first point—the role of the library and the librarian—and the other subjects are given only superficial treatment. I am insisting that the college student needs and should be given a sound education in these matters, and especially, perhaps, in the use of the card catalog. This matter of the catalog I am sure needs further defense, and in any case it is time that some strong words were uttered on the virtues rather than the deficiencies of that much-maligned instrument. If you will permit a small digression, then, which nevertheless is related to the central problem, I should like to say that I frequently have been irritated by sweeping attacks on the card catalog. It seems strange to me that this tool, which provides the sole reliable key to the particular collection it describes, should be referred to as an "obstacle" or a "barrier." Is an index a barrier to the contents of a book? Or a street directory a barrier to locating a given house in a city? Or is the art of reading a barrier to understanding what is printed? The barrier is not in the thing itself, but in the incomprehension of the person who cannot use the key provided.

There is one other point to be considered when we are talking about the catalog in relation to student use, and especially when we are thinking about modifying it to suit student abilities. We may forget, or fail to perceive, that the librarian's primary duty, in constructing and maintaining his catalog, is not to the user of the collection but to the collection itself. In discharging his cataloging obligation he must be governed first by what is necessary in relation to the mass of recorded knowledge he is attempting to control. In other words, while he must, of course, consider those who will use his catalog, he must never permit the weaknesses or ignorance of that clientele to sway him from doing whatever is necessary to impose the requisite bibliographical control on the collection in his charge. This is particularly important when both knowledge and libraries are growing so rapidly. As a matter of fact, of course, the more highly refined a catalog becomes and the more liberal the entries and modes of approach provided, the more useful it becomes. And, for-

tunately, once the user understands the basic principles upon which a catalog is constructed, the difficulty of using it does not increase with its size. All of which constitutes, it seems to me, another reason for training the student up to the use of the catalog.

Thus far I have largely ignored, as I am sure you have realized, a whole set of library aims and a plethora of vigorous library activities based upon them. These are the aims which have to do with the encouragement of recreational reading, with the instillation of the reading habit, and with the development of a love for books. I have elected to treat separately of these aims and their attendant functions because I think that such treatment will emphasize my major points. I should like to call these aims "unofficial," and for two reasons. First, they seem to me to be at least a step removed from the academic library's main task of implementing the course of instruction and the work of the faculty. Second, I call them "unofficial" in the sense that they represent a set of purposes that have been established and developed almost solely through the initiative of librarians. I suspect that many college instructors are puzzled by the emphasis given such library aims and functions and that their support, if they give it at all, is based upon the largely visceral notion that anything intended to promote the use of books must be "good." It is difficult to document this statement, but a number of faculty members, from institutions other than my own, have said to me despairingly that they sometimes wished librarians would quit harping about nonreading students and non-library-conscious faculty members; and they have gone on to indicate that the curriculum and their assignments are demanding enough fully to occupy the student's time. There is some point in this. In one sense the college is competing against its course of study and its faculty. The school sponsors athletic programs, dramatic activities, musical events, student clubs and committees, and a hundred other enterprises that, all together, take a substantial amount of the student's time when he is not in class—or even when he should be. There are grounds for putting the library's recreational reading campaigns in this category of damaging (educationally speaking) activities.

On the other hand, the encouragement of the habit of reading and the stimulation of a love for books do seem to be logical extensions of the purposes of the liberal arts college. We seem to have here an unfortunate dualism, with the library and the faculty both working toward the same general goals, but with the library working independently and elaborating a function that may in many ways detract from the work of one of the primary instruments of the college. It could be argued, from a superficial point of view, that the library has stepped in because the faculty has failed in this particular area. Or it can be argued, with more justification, that the faculty has deliberately left it to the library to develop the love of books and the habit of reading. I should like to suggest another answer, using as my springboard a remark made earlier in this discussion.

I said, some pages ago, that attitudes must be inculcated. I said also, in defining the liberal arts, that the third aim of the college was to give the student "what amounts to an incidental by-product but is the most valuable of all—a sense of values." The habit of reading and the love of books are attitudes, and a preference for books and reading is the exercise of a sense of values. We know too

little about how attitudes or values are established, but we do know that many influences operate to this end. We can also safely assume, I think, that they flow far more frequently from the home and other early influences and from persons or groups of persons (among whom I am willing to include teachers and librarians) than they do from things or collections of things or from books read. There are grounds for thinking that these qualities which librarians try so hard to instil are already in the student when he arrives on campus or that they are developed, where they are developed at all, from stimuli received in the classroom, the faculty offices, and the dormitory.

If there is truth in this view, perhaps the faculty has not ignored or abandoned one of its functions, but rather has seen, felt, or assumed that the function is carried out automatically and without emphasis—an intangible by-product of the more tangible activities of the college. To accept this position is not necessarily to say that the library should not consciously play a part in stimulating an interest in books and in reading. It does suggest, however, that the librarian as a person may be far more influential than the luxuriously furnished reading-rooms and the invitingly arranged shelves. And this in turn suggests that the chief librarian might put his money into staff rather than into special undergraduate collections.

It is at this point, I think, that we come finally to the real difference between the college and the university library. And the difference is not in the size of the library or in the research characteristics of the library's collections. The significant difference lies outside the library itself; it is to be found in the size and the nature of the small, independent college, as opposed to the size and nature of the college attached to the large university. If, as I have just been saying, attitudes and a sense of values are the products of personal stimulation, of faculty attitudes, of "atmosphere," as it were, then the good, small independent liberal arts college—and I wish to emphasize the first modifier—the *good*, small liberal arts college clearly is better able to stimulate and develop such attitudes and values than is the college attached to the large university. There may be exceptions, but, in general, the college in a large university tends to be characterized by large classes, impersonal instruction, and a bare minimum of student-faculty association outside the scheduled class hours. The undergraduate student body, too, is likely to have far less cohesion and homogeneity and far fewer opportunities for rewarding intellectual exchange among its members. In the good, independent college the opposite is likely to be the case, and, as President Davidson remarked in his paper, it is this climate of intimacy to which the small liberal arts college owes its virtues and its continuing existence.

The problem, then, is that in the small, independent college the elements necessary for the instillation of the desired attitudes and values are likely to exist, while in the college attached to the large university the elements are likely not to exist. Is this not what the university librarian is worrying about when he wonders whether he should supply separate undergraduate facilities? He is seeking to fill a gap which in the large institution may not, after all, be imaginary. He is not the person primarily responsible for filling that gap. That is the responsibility of the university and the college authorities, who should strive to create an atmosphere more friendly

to the instillation of these intangible by-products we have been talking about. This means a smaller faculty-student ratio and, if possible, a more intimate living and learning situation for the undergraduate students. If the college or university administration cannot provide these and similar resources, then the library remains as an alternative device, and, given an adequate budget, the librarian may be able to offer within the library that personal stimulation which the large college itself cannot. He can do so, however, only at the expenditure of a considerable sum of money above and beyond what he must expend for a staff trained for good, conventional library service; and even after this expenditure his efforts will represent only an imperfect substitute.

The program I have outlined in the first part of this paper—the thorough and continuing instruction on libraries and their use—would, if carried out in the fashion I have described, answer many of these unfilled needs in the university-attached college. I am willing to grant, however, that in the large college we are likely never to have the degree of personal association that obtains in the good liberal arts college. I can therefore see some grounds for special provision for undergraduate students—the university librarian filling the gap.

He can best do this, I have already indicated, by putting his money into staff rather than into separate undergraduate facilities. But by *staff* I do not mean a few more reference or circulation librarians. I mean competent, interested, professional persons, sufficiently numerous to have the time to work with undergraduates, sufficiently sympathetic to attract the students, and sufficiently learned to make the association meaningful. It will be their mission to provide the personal stimulation that may otherwise be lacking, and, above all, as I have suggested elsewhere in some earlier remarks on this general subject, to make certain that they and the faculty together find all the true readers or potential readers in the undergraduate population and that they see that these students get the books they want and whatever special treatment may be desirable—the opportunity to discuss these books and broaden their reading and grow intellectually to the limits of their natural endowment.

It may be necessary or desirable to provide a headquarters for this staff—a point to which undergraduates will turn —but in my opinion it would be unwise to divorce this area physically from the university library itself. In some situations it may be necessary or expedient to create separate facilities and a separate collection; but I feel that the student has so much to gain by being required to use a large collection that I regard a separate, selected library as a poor second choice. (I might insert here that I have little quarrel with Lamont; to argue against Lamont, with its collection of close to 100,000 volumes, is to argue against the idea of a library itself. Even with that large collection, however, the Harvard undergraduate must still use the other Harvard libraries on occasion, and one may wonder whether he should not be trained for such use from the very beginning of his collegiate career.)

Free access to the book stock, too, is not a substitute for instruction in the use of the library or for a really good staff. I favor free access, and I would urge libraries of all sizes to allow it wherever possible; but none of us should entertain any notion that the freedom to range through a great, or even a relatively small, collection of books will very often lead to a program of systematic reading. It is quite as likely to lead to a fruitless dissipation of time. Its one virtue is the introduction it affords to many titles and many ideas; it builds up, as it were, an *allusion bank*. This is important and something difficult to come by in any other way; but in itself—without the discipline of systematic study—it can also be a dangerous diversion.

Let me now attempt to tie together all that I have said in this long discourse. I have suggested that the question whether the university library is able to serve the undergraduate cannot be looked at solely in terms of size, the nature of the book collection, or the other commitments of the large institution. The problem must be considered in the light of the educational needs of the college student; and, when this is done, the university library is seen to have potential advantages over the college library. The realization of these potentialities is dependent, however, upon the student's possession of knowledge and skill in library matters—a complex of abilities that I have suggested constitutes one of the liberal arts. The most important desideratum, therefore, is thoroughgoing instruction in this art.

Since, however, the instruction is requisite whether the student be enrolled in the independent college or in the college attached to the large university, the administration of that instruction might seem to leave the advantage with the student who is served by the larger university library. This is true, however, only with respect to the two more tangible aims of the liberal arts college. In the area of the intangible values the advantage may lie the other way, and the university library may possibly have to compensate, not for its own size, complexity, and impersonality, but for the size and impersonality of the university-attached college itself.

Where does this leave the university librarian? The first step he (and all librarians) must take, the first long battle he and they must fight, is to see to it that the college curriculum provides adequate formal instruction in the role of the library and the processes by which society's memory is made usable and that the teaching methods require sufficient constructive, repeated use of the library to insure that the students become proficient in the art. I see no other way to give students that knowledge and those skills, and I suspect also that there is no more effective way to instil the habit of reading and the habit of turning to books for continuing education.

The second step is the provision of the competent, interested professional staff I described a few moments ago. We must have such a staff in any event (and few of us have it now); but if we are also to compensate in part for a small and overworked faculty, we must build an even larger and more able group of librarians.

These, then, are the essentials: the books themselves, the guides to the books, the instruction in library purposes and techniques, and the staff. What the university librarian may do beyond this in the way of special facilities depends upon the financial support available and also, unfortunately, upon the dictates of expedience. But whatever is done should be done with the educational needs of the student and with the aims of the college firmly in mind. If the essentials are provided, the university library will be performing, in a significant and influential manner, its liberal arts functions.

THE NATURE OF THE COLLEGE-LIBRARY BOOK COLLECTION

NEWTON F. McKEON

THE question implied by my subject is very simply asked. Allowing for ambiguity, it can be stated as two questions: What books do college libraries have? and What books should they have? The answer to the first is descriptive and, for present purposes, unprofitable to pursue, save as it bears on the second question. The answer to the second is quickly and easily given. The book stock should, of course, be appropriate to its purpose and comprise books of the first quality. Can anyone dissent? Yet, like the story about Jack a Nory and the sequel concerning Jack and his brother, this is open to the objection that it consciously avoids the question.

A library's book collection is its essential element. No matter how skilled the staff or how satisfactory the plant, a library with a poor collection is inevitably committed to mediocrity and ineffectiveness. Therefore, the clearest possible answer to the question which has just been begged is of very great importance. But, on the one hand, lies the general, abounding in clichés and approving metaphors. They must be avoided, in that they only lead on to more and more verbalisms, no matter how fresh and bright and ingenious. On the other hand, lies the specific, in its purest form the list. What could be more definite and particular and satisfying than a list of the best books for the college library? And how dreary for you and for me. But lists will mislead as badly as words. A list would falsely imply that colleges are the same in all respects,

that what is good for one is good for all. We know otherwise.

So the problem is to speak to the point, steadfastly avoiding these two extremes. This is made difficult by the literature on the subject which already exists. It is extensive and, taken together, exhaustive. No aspect of the college-library book collection but has had its commentators, perceptive, wise, cranky, pedestrian, and trivial. "Of making many books there is no end; and much study is a weariness of the flesh." Of the making of many statements about books gathered in libraries, the same may be said. I approach this task with hesitation, aware that what remains to be said is less a matter of substance than of emphasis, of angle of vision, and, unavoidably, of implied autobiography.

First, it is necessary to sharpen the focus. The remarks which follow are confined to the library of the indigenous and traditional four-year liberal arts college, as distinguished from all other undergraduate institutions bearing the name "college." They, furthermore, presume to use the word "books" in the broadest sense, without paying heed to the present wide variety of their form. Finally, they deal only with the stock of books, ignoring financing, processing, arranging, describing, and all the other factors which influence a library collection. With this underbrush cut away, it is now possible to rephrase the original question: How, in this day of the proliferation of "subjects," of floods of print greater than ever before, of the bewitching and despairing phrase "bibliographical control," of costs which rise and rise, are college libraries to plot their course in building and managing their collections?

Those colleges of which I speak are many in number and scattered widely throughout the country. Their enrolments continue to be small; their control and finances are independent. They persist in devoting themselves primarily to liberal education despite the advent of general education and the enticements of the vocational. The particular contribution they are able to make to a confused democracy in a troubled world cannot be overemphasized. In its recent report, *The Nature and Needs of Higher Education*, the Commission on Financing Higher Education observes that a liberal education "lies at the very heart of all higher education . . . [it] is education in the art of being free. By definition it would be anathema to dictatorship." This is a high responsibility with which to be charged. If it is to be fulfilled, the libraries of liberal arts colleges are required to play a very important part. Here, if anywhere, is justification for speaking now on a well-worn subject.

Lest these seem no more than large, empty words, let us consider briefly the findings of some recent studies on the contribution of the liberal arts colleges. In 1947 the Steelman report, *Science and Public Policy*, investigated those undergraduate institutions which produced successful candidates for the Ph.D. in sciences and discovered that 39 of the 44 ranking institutions were colleges, 3 were universities, and 2 were technical schools. Knapp and Goodrich, studying what they termed "the production of scientists" five years later, reported that the 50 leading institutions comprised 33 liberal arts colleges, 16 universities, and 1 technical school.[1] The broader study,

The Young American Scholar: His Collegiate Origins, of Knapp and Greenbaum, which appeared last year, was not confined to scientists. It found that the highest 50 institutions "in distinction" included 31 liberal arts colleges, 12 private universities, 4 public universities, and 3 technical schools. This evidence is cited not to laud the colleges of liberal arts but to remind ourselves of the paradox that the "impractical" training of liberal education does, indeed, prepare its students to take their places in our technological, professional, pragmatic world.

Each liberal arts college stands alone, without benefit of the public purse, an integer, not a fraction of a university. Situated usually in a small town, often extremely isolated not only from urban centers but from institutional neighbors, it must necessarily provide itself generously with library resources. But self-sufficiency is not the only resaon for its requiring the best library it can afford. The education it provides demands of the students a more intimate and more extensive contact with books than does any other. Its faculty has perhaps a deeper involvement in its library than do other faculties. Books at such institutions are pre-eminently the chief instruments of instruction. "A liberal education . . . is concerned with ideas, with all kinds of ideas, good, bad or indifferent."[2] This requires books in some profusion for the teachers and the taught.

Much has been said on the subject of the size of the college-library book collection. Here is a very red herring, for it diverts attention from considerations of

[1] R. H. Knapp and H. B. Goodrich, *Origins of American Scientists* (Chicago: University of Chicago Press, 1952), p. 22.

[2] Commission on Financing Higher Education, *Nature and Needs of Higher Education* . . . (New York: Columbia University Press, 1952), p. 103.

quality to those of quantity. Such a very persistent topic for pronouncements must be confronted. As few as 10,000 volumes have been declared sufficient for a college library. Numerous larger estimates have been made, none, be it remarked, approaching the actual size of a number of college libraries today. Are we to infer from this that these libraries, in exceeding what are deemed reasonable bounds, have gotten out of hand and have become unwieldy, inefficient, too good for their purposes, or too fraught with the lumber of the unusable?

Some of the prescriptions as to desirable size have come from those associated with liberal arts colleges, persons intimately concerned with the management, financing, and effective operation of their libraries—President Davidson, for example. But more often they have been suggested by university librarians. Can it be that, with the best will in the world, they have not known what they were talking about? From the university Olympus the liberal college may appear very insignificant, or possibly it can too easily be equated with the university's own undergraduate college, with the consequence that its library may, perhaps, seem to be, or need to be, little more than a glorified reserve-book room.

The original Chicago college library of 2,000 titles in 12,000 volumes has stood as an example of the extreme lower limit in size. Today we are all conscious of Lamont's 39,000-odd titles limited to a total of 100,000 volumes, particularly so since its catalog has been made available in book form and college librarians are all wondering what they can usefully learn from it. Both these libraries assume the propinquity and availability of university library resources. Each is squarely addressed to its own clearly defined local obligations. Each is a "good" library for its purposes. Yet neither provides a pattern which a liberal arts college library can safely follow, for both have been able to escape the essential obligation of providing for their faculties.

But the question of how large a college-library book collection should be still remains. The only answer possible is that it should be as large as the educational objectives of its institution require and, within the limits set by them, as large as the college can afford, as large as it can be and still perform effectively the functions asked of it. This is said not without a full awareness that growth (and hence size) is the incubus above us all and that the pains of growth are as acute for the libraries of colleges as for those of universities. Were it of consequence to try to determine the desirable size for a given library at a given point in time, many factors would have to enter the calculation, among them: the faculty and its interests and quality, the students and theirs, the scope and distribution of the curriculum, the prevailing intellectual climate, the presence or absence of pressures for "productive scholarship," the prevailing methods of instruction. But this is to anticipate the central consideration of the nature of the collection, which is inextricably connected with demand and use. To conclude the subject of size, let me say with Keogh: "Number of volumes means little more than their cubage or their weight; it is appropriateness, it is quality, that counts."[3]

Quality is surely the key word to employ in attempting to state what is desired in the collection, not solely the qual-

[3] A. Keogh, "Address at the Dedication of the Sterling Memorial Library at Yale University on 11 April 1931," *Yale University Library Gazette*, V (April, 1931), 134.

ity which inheres in a particular book but equally the quality of appropriateness of a body of books to their purpose. This is sound doctrine for any library. We hear continually that what is wanted are good, live, worth-while, great, important, substantial, basic books of merit and character. The good books, that is, in distinction from the poor books. We hear, too, of the need for useful, suitable, effective, carefully or correctly selected books. These are the appropriate books, the best books for the purpose at hand. We all subscribe to the desirability of striving to round out or build up or develop a well-distributed and strong collection which, at the least, should be adequate and, at the best, rich. But this is the treacherous verbal terrain which was to be avoided. It invites only to ingenuities of synonym and metaphor which create the illusion of light without illuminating. What is required instead is some degree of specification as to the characteristics and elements of a college library's book collection. And to bedevil this task, as the Introduction to the catalog of the Lamont Library accurately observes, "if a college library should reflect the aims and educational policy of its institution, the diversity of aims among our colleges militates against identical book collections." Perhaps, since liberal arts colleges have a common aim, it were more accurate to have said "diversity of means."

Before any college library can hope to determine what its collection should be, certain questions must be asked and answered. Does the curriculum strictly limit the library's area of responsibility? If it does not, by virtue of what authority, decision, or policy is the field of operation deemed to be wider? Does the library have an obligation to local needs only? Or is it expected to make some contribution to cultural resources on a regional or national or international scale? Does the library purpose to serve undergraduate students primarily? Or is the library to be principally directed toward the faculty? Or toward both? To what extent, if any, is the library to be regarded as an independent teaching agency, encouraging and promoting the use of books in ways beyond those suggested or required by the classroom? Or is the library auxiliary to the teaching and learning on the campus and no more?

The college library which regards itself in more than strictly local institutional terms suffers delusions of grandeur. Its task is clearly and simply to serve its own institution to the fullest possible extent. The needs of both students and faculty must be supplied as well and as amply as the best available judgment directs and the funds at hand permit. Emulation, prestige, megalomania, are all foreign to this clear obligation.

If it be asked how this goal is to be approached, attention must first be directed to the faculty, which in a liberal arts college is its library's principal shaping force. As teachers, faculty members necessarily have the responsibility for determining student use of the library. As collaborators with the library, they (those devoted members who have a natural instinct impelling them) select the books to be acquired in the subjects comprised in the curriculum. As scholars, they make the heaviest demands on its resources. It is not too much to say that a college library is as good as the faculty it serves. A "good" library and a mediocre faculty are a contradiction. A "poor" library and a superior faculty are a contradiction. Quality in the one begets comparable quality in the other. An administration which has succeeded in assembling a superior faculty incurs thereby the obligation to spend handsomely for library purposes. Self-interest dictates to an institution in this happy situation that a very large factor in retaining this faculty and in making appointments and replacements to it is found in the nature of the library resources made available.

Teaching is the college's particular enterprise. The library exists in order to support this teaching. From this follows the inescapable fact that the library is an adjunct, the essential adjunct, to teaching, and its obligation is to follow where teaching leads. This is not to deny that the librarian and the staff have a very heavy obligation to be as informed and as active as they possibly can in making their domain the most effective ally of the classroom. But it is to assert that no college library can hope to attain its purposes if it conceives of itself as a sovereign realm living an autonomous existence, simply another department fighting its way, asserting its independence, in the midst of departmentalism. Here is no argument for supineness or passivity, but a reminder that the library has a heavy responsibility, in the discharge of which it is hampered if, by obtuseness, it mistakes itself for what it is not. Faculty and library must make common cause if education matters.

Here it becomes necessary to confront a misleading distinction commonly made between teachers and scholars. In preparation for their careers, college teachers and university teachers

... were nursed upon the self-same hill
Fed the same flock by fountain, shade, and rill.

No one would be so bold as to claim that only the scholars *manqués* take college teaching posts. Scholarship is a continu-

ing activity for the intellectually able teacher wherever he may be, whether or not it emerges as publication. College teachers "drank of Avon, too, a dang'rous draught." They may be depended upon to continue to be students unremittingly, if they are to teach well, students of their own field, amateurs of many others. They can say with the poet:

But yield who will to their separation
My object in living is to unite
My avocation and my vocation
As my two eyes make one in sight.

As for the occasional professor who makes a career of warming and rewarming his old lecture notes, whose sustenance is his own accumulated mental fat, he does not concern the library. He is his president's problem.

What need is there, then, to state the obvious, that the college library has a particular obligation to supply teachers with the working materials for scholarship in their fields? The day of the scholar's private working library on the nineteenth-century Germanic model, has long gone by. Today the impecunious teacher contrives to make ends meet by economizing at the expense of his library and his wardrobe. Under these conditions the responsibility of the college library to supply unstintingly the books he requires is greater than ever before. A skilled workman must be furnished with tools of the best quality and with all the varieties of tools he needs if his best work is to be done.

The journal, the proceedings, the transactions, are the principal means of intercommunication which scholars employ. Such publications, in all the fields pertinent to the curriculum, must be secured by the library in full measure. The subjects embraced in the liberal arts curriculum are relatively few in number and broad, rather than highly specialized, in scope. This helps place limits on the library's responsibilities for such materials. Many fields of study can be ignored, others which are cognate need to be represented in only a skeleton fashion. This is one point, perhaps it is *the* point, of difference between the college and the university library: the former is perforce far more selective. Nevertheless, the responsibility for journals which it must assume remains a heavy one.

But it is not sufficient that a faculty be enabled to keep currently apprised of scholarship in the areas of its interest. If study is to be made possible, particularly in fields other than science, source material must be at hand. Depending upon the use to which it is put, almost any book may be called a source. The word is not employed here in that wide sense. What is intended to be signified are major compilations of original material, definitive works, official documents, society publications, reprinting manuscripts and texts, and the like—the books themselves, not the books about them or the books about the books about them. Some appear serially, some are published as sets, some, such as government documents, are profuse outpourings of printed matter. This category, needless to say, is not distinct from that of journals. We all are aware of how *De Bow's Review* or the *Gentleman's Magazine* serve as sources for studies in their periods. Such materials have this in common: they are substantial in bulk or cost, or both, and they contain the essential ore which scholarship works. Furthermore, and to be specific, United Nations documents, Hansard, Migne, the "Rolls Series," the Corpuses (or Corpora) of whatever variety, the Selden Society, Defoe's *Review*, Jefferson's *Papers*, do not constitute an inventory

which will have a rapid turnover in use. Yet, though costly, though often massive, though infrequently used, materials such as these may be depended upon to be enduringly useful. Obviously, what has already been said of journals applies with double force to source materials: there must be a high selectivity in their acquisition.

For a liberal arts college to offer individual advanced work, under whatever name or plan, to upper-class students, lacking in its library extensive files of appropriate journals and selected sources, is incomprehensible. This culmination of a liberal arts education, requiring the use of basic sources, is the best of what a college has to offer its students. It provides an opportunity for them to attempt on a limited scale what their preceptors do when they engage in scholarship. If the experience is to be rewarding, the library resources which help to make it possible must be the best that can be had. This amounts to saying that books of the type under discussion are essential for student as well as for faculty use. Their acquisition is emphatically not a matter of playing the sedulous ape to the university or of blind devotion to long-accepted custom.

To satisfy myself that this is not empty talk, I have examined the bibliographies of a sample lot of senior honors theses accepted at Amherst in the last ten years. In them was to be found, in addition to journal references in profusion, evidence of wide employment of federal documents, including volumes in the congressional set, legislative committee hearings, the Nürnberg trials, the *Congressional Record, Annals of Congress,* and the *Congressional Globe.* There appeared seventeenth- and eighteenth-century books, never reprinted, such as Eden's *State of the Poor*, Arthur

Young's *Tours* and *Travels*, Rushworth's *Historical Collection of Private Passages of State*. Then followed Hansard, the Historical Manuscripts Commission, the *New York Times*, local newspapers. This running recital points in large part to work in history and the social sciences. In the sciences, as far as texts were required, journals supplied all needs. Theses in the humanities depended most heavily upon the best texts of the authors under study. This is clearly an area in which a college library must plan to be strong—the works of major writers and selected minor writers in the most satisfactory editions and in all the fields of study offered.

Since a college library is committed to selectivity in its resources, a strong reference collection is essential. Full utilization of the very materials which have just been indicated at some length is impossible without a plentiful supply of reference books. This needs no demonstration. Yet, if we consider Winchell, we return again to what at this point is the theme of this discourse—selectivity. Patently, the possession of everything listed there would be an absurdity for a college library; yet a generous share of all that is appropriate and promises to be useful is cardinal.

No less vital is bibliography in the widest sense of the term. It is justly said that knowing where to find a particular book is as good as owning it. Unsparing outlays for this purpose will bring returns perennially. The library committed to possessing what is only a very small portion of the world's books needs particularly to have the means of knowing about those other books which it chose not to have, or could not afford, or unwittingly rejected in the decision to acquire what it did acquire. Now that we have it and have become accustomed to depending upon it, we wonder how we

ever managed without Donald Wing's *Short Title Catalogue*, to cite one example. The same can be said of so many of our bibliographical aids, old as well as new.

What has been said up to this point about the essential elements of a college-library collection implies a very onerous charge on a limited book budget. If journals and sources and books of reference and bibliography are to be acquired on the handsome scale recommended, will funds be left for other purposes? Can any newly published books relevant to the subjects of instruction be afforded? Of course, they must be acquired, but only after balancing the need for them against the need for all these other materials. The necessity to make such judgments presses with particular acuteness on every college library today, not only to make the judgments but to be ready to revise them with increasing frequency. The rising costs of the serials and sets which are indispensable encroach progressively upon book funds, to the point where they threaten to pre-empt them. Unless faculty members and librarians can face this problem together with openness and understanding, irreparable harm may be done the collections.

The elements of the collection still to be mentioned are three: duplicates, books for those who read simply because they like to, and rare books. The duplication of books which many students are required to read is an important matter. Too long and too generally there has prevailed among college librarians a tendency to deplore, to decry, to resist, and to lament the employment of their funds for this purpose. Why buy a second copy when the purchase money would acquire a new title? This is a taboo which needs to be proscribed. If the method of teaching requires whole classes to read the same assignment (a most laudable attempt to escape from the single textbook), the library is perverse and remiss if it fails to make adequate (not insufficient or grudging) provision for such demand. Just as a laboratory equips itself with a battery of microscopes (all identical), so that each experimenter in his turn may have the equipment he needs, so must the library prepare to meet the demand made upon it by the classroom. If this seems costly, a corrective is to be found by considering the salary of a laboratory assistant, which is similarly an instruction cost.

Next comes the provision to be made for the general reader. The college library which has been described thus far may sound a little forbidding when we consider the person who naturally reads books, who has a taste for ranging freely, without guidance, among books which are neither collateral nor required. Provision must assuredly be made for him, outnumbered though he may be by his fellows whose literacy does not incline them to consort with books save under compulsion. The habitual reader of brummagem books is another matter. For him a sort of Gresham's Law obtains whereby bad books drive out good books. The college library must not pander to him. In providing for the natural reader there must be no debasement or lowering of standards. Fastidious selectivity for this purpose is essential. But, granted this, there must be attained, in so far as possible, a fine excess, a generous supply, various and full of possible surprises, discoveries, and delights, allowing full play for serendipity to operate, a plentiful show of the wealth and splendor of books.

And now a word about rare books. The college library without a representation, however slight and unpretentious, of fine and distinguished books is necessarily impoverished. In a setting where the love of books is shared, albeit with varying degrees of intensity, by teacher, librarian, and student, it is most desirable to have at hand the means to illustrate the history of the book, to display examples of significant contributions in the history of man's thought, or to exhibit the book as an object of beauty. Yet funds furnished to sustain a useful working library are misapplied if they are employed for this purpose in any but the most chary fashion. For such possessions the library must look primarily to donors. Even so, a rare-book collection must be kept within bounds and not be allowed to grow to proportions which incur a heavy burden of maintenance. If it cannot be brought into play for instruction or delight, however, it becomes an unwarranted luxury. Above all, a college library must not be deluded into overvaluing what it calls its rare books. They are not likely to cohere into a body of material which can serve scholarship. A little knowledge of important private and institutional collections is certain to dim the luster which local pride of possession may beget.

The tale of the college library's contents has now been told. The next object of our concern must be their growth. Practical (and very compelling) considerations aside, it is wholly irrational to contemplate a future in which college-library collections grow larger each year. In this process, at some point which will differ for each library, an optimum size is certain to be attained, for this growth is the only variable among a group of constants: enrolment, faculty, curriculum. I propose to approach the problem of growth and its control obliquely by reverting first to some aspects of book selection which remain to be considered.

It has been assumed that the largest part of the responsibility for book selection is delegated to the faculty. Waiting, then, for each book which has been ordered is a person who saw a use for it and can be expected to employ it when it reaches him. With gifts the situation is otherwise. They do not come to answer a felt need or an expressed desire. Therefore, they must be scrutinized by the library with extreme care. To adapt a familiar saying: Never accession what you can't use because it is free. Welcome though gifts are, useful though some of them can be, the library has a pressing responsibility to protect itself unceasingly from them. This means accepting gifts of books without condition, and keeping only those which can be employed. The tests to which all gifts must be subjected are such as these: Is this a book we would have chosen to purchase? Is this a book which So-and-So can put to use? Does this complement present resources so as to add to their effectiveness?

The greatest asset a college library has in assuring discriminating book selection is the limit of its funds. Everyone concerned in ordering is aware that choosing this means foregoing that. This enforces an element of deliberation and hence a more careful selection than would be made if finances seemed ampler. Beyond this are other assets which do not obtain, as it were, automatically, but must be cultivated. Since the participants in book selection are many, their independent efforts must, as far as possible, be made into team play. For this there must be wide faculty good will toward the library, making possible the maximum collaboration. There should be an alert, informed librarian and staff, who understand the curriculum, the personalities of the faculty, their interests and their methods. The library should not be passive, but active, picking the brains and soliciting the participation of faculty members of all ranks, encouraging them to take a stake in the

library. The resulting community of interest and sense of common cause are powerful factors in achieving a better library.

But for all this, is not the total situation basically random and chaotic? Is there to be no plan of selection? To this an honest answer must be: Very little. A library worth its salt is continuously scrutinizing itself, more by intuition than methodically, observing its strengths and weaknesses. Out of this knowledge come actions, many of them insignificant—a conversation here, a suggestion there, an inquiry about unfilled needs, a dealer's catalogue forwarded, a purchase made. This is an undramatic sort of retrospective planning, if you will, but it seems to be the way in which order and proportion are sought after for the collection. To absolve himself, as it were, from appearing to be on false ground, to ridicule gently the earnest and sober-faced advocates of a "Book Selection Plan," the candid librarian of a very great college library has written: "There is probably some curiosity as to how this library has been built up, whether there has been a plan. If by this is meant a continuous organized effort to study the bibliography of all fields, and keep them fairly abreast, there has not. Perhaps there should have been, though no one seemed to have the time."[4] Further candor compels the admission that this practice, which prevails widely, permits many tares to invade the wheat and creates a growth which invites future culling.

The acquisition and preservation of books are beset by a number of taboos, pitfalls, fetishes, and *idées fixes* which hamper and bedevil. The distaste for the purchase of duplicates has already

[4] N. L. G[oodrich], "Pleasures of Selection," *Dartmouth College Library Bulletin*, II (December, 1937), 159.

been mentioned. This springs from a worthy motive, the insistent desire to be ever building a stronger collection. But it ignores convenience, as well as obligations to users. A case could be made for greater willingness to duplicate for other uses than the reserve shelves. Quite possibly time study and cost analysis would show that a second set of the *Library of Congress Catalog*, for example, strategically placed might more than pay for itself in the time and energy thus saved both staff and public. A second attitude to be countered is hesitancy over a purchase which seems expensive. This does not afflict science or art departments, both conditioned to think in terms of large costs by the other materials and equipment with which they deal. But for other disciplines this deterrent grows stronger each year as the cost of books increases. Here the librarian must encourage and hearten and tempt and be prepared to underwrite. A substantial work promising to endure, however costly, is far to be preferred to the indiscriminate accumulating of modestly priced secondary works. Then there is the persuasive authority of the selected list and the bibliography, which must be resisted. Using them for buying purposes without exercising over them the most careful selection means thralldom, the abdication of judgment, indiscriminate reliance on authority, often costly and needless competition in the book market, and inevitably leads to the acquisition of materials which are not needed. This danger is closely allied to the librarian's occupational malady, the itch for completeness, for "coverage." This is a wholly irrational inclination, most beguiling because it is so easy to yield to, so appealing to neat-mindedness, but altogether at variance with the principle of selectivity which must prevail for a college library. Pargellis illustrates the point at issue well when he says that, of 3,500–4,000 distinct books about Lincoln, there are perhaps 70 good ones.[5] The college library therefore does not use Monaghan as a buying list, nor does it write to ask that the 70 books be listed. It employs its best judgment to select with the discrimination which Pargellis implies is necessary.

To continue this recital of hazards, we must next consider satisfaction over size; the unwise acceptance of gifts; the credo that everything written is worth preserving and ultimately has its use; the vague, tacit assumption that on each library fall some obligations of stewardship for the world of learning at large; the fear of discarding what may be the last surviving copy; the humility which suggests that you are not omniscient and may be wrong in judging against a book. Together, these inhibitions and compulsions work against selectivity very powerfully by bringing into the collection books which need not be there and by making their later excision as difficult as possible. For selection does not end with the decision to acquire a book. Retrospective selection is as important to a college library as is current selection. Continuous reappraisal of resources deserves to be put upon a regularly organized basis and not left to be a spasmodic or emergency operation, as it usually is. As Miss McCrum has pointed out, the best books do not cause the problem of growth. Our mistakes do that in large part.[6] Some are caused by the attitudes and habits which have just been noted. Others are the result of bad judgment which has allowed inferior or useless books to creep in. The work of

[5] S. Pargellis, "Some Remarks on Bibliography," *College and Research Libraries*, VII (July, 1946), 207.

[6] B. P. McCrum, "Book Selection in Relation to the Optimum Size of a College Library," *College and Research Libraries*, XI (April, 1950), 139.

time is another thing, when good books are supplanted by better books or when occasional and topical books, having served their immediate purpose, become outmoded.

There is observable in many quarters a marked aversion for the term "weeding." This has led to the employment of such a monstrous euphemism as "collection evaluation." The figure of a garden under cultivation implied by *weeding* is homely, appropriate, and should be entirely satisfying. Weeding is difficult; good weeding comes high, for it demands the best skill available; the press of other more insistent daily matters seems to leave no time or energy for it. Yet to college librarians I would say: take courage, dare to risk appearing to be an enemy of books, determinedly do away with the inappropriate and the ineffective, admit no responsibility for retaining books other than those demonstrably useful to the institution your library serves. Even if you make errors, a little attrition of the vast bulk of print now in library custody may be more beneficial than harmful. Unless you do take measures, "open stack" will become in the end an empty phrase, as the weeds crowd in about the desired growths. Here a *caveat* is needed. Much can be said for the presence of some poor books if they are recognized for what they are. Since education involves learning to discriminate, they have their uses.

But weeding alone will not control growth, though it does help to curb it. Where weeding ends, co-operation may safely begin. For the college library, one is the corollary of the other. Together they provide the only hopeful attack on the problem of growth. One is a means of eliminating what is judged to be of no use; the other imposes some measure of control upon the resources which are esteemed. This is an important distinction, because co-operative efforts which are directed toward what is little-valued or ill-considered are misbegotten and wholly wasteful. When all possible pruning has been done, the books which remain will be of two sorts: those in active use and those infrequently required. At the necessary price of foregoing immediacy, co-operation can go far in coping on a rational basis with the latter.

Co-operation we know can usefully take many forms. It can be tacit and informal, as when one library, aware of resources within reach, purposely refrains from duplication. Or it can be based upon engagements formally made. These can be as various as the needs and circumstances of the participants recommend. Whatever form it takes, co-operation involves a collaborative approach to a set of highly individual situations and requires the sacrifice of some autonomy in order to attain the desired results. In so far as co-operation has been profitably practiced, it has demonstrated that it can substantially affect the nature of a collection, in terms of both current acquisitions and retrospective holdings. Agreements governing responsibility for acquisitions work to this end in one direction, those relating to the deposit of material in another.

Co-operation is a large subject in itself. In order not to digress at length from the main subject, I must assume that its literature, its achievements, and its future possibilities are a matter of general knowledge. However, the statements which have been made deserve some illustration if they are to carry conviction. This can best be drawn from firsthand experience. It is my good fortune to be associated with neighbor college librarians in a co-operative venture, which is proving to be perhaps the most exciting library task to which we have put our hands. Our little acorn is far from having become a great oak, but we are assiduously cultivating a sturdy young seedling, which promises to thrive. We see in our joint efforts such goals as these: the curbing of needless duplication both current and past, the attainment of richer total resources, radical curtailment of future book-storage needs, insurance against the harmful effects of rising costs, particularly those for subscriptions.

To illustrate how these are being sought, reference to a group of mathematical journals will serve very well. Three mathematics departments examined their current journal subscriptions, concentrating attention on highly specialized publications. They fixed on three (one Danish, one Dutch, one French), for each of which a single subscription was deemed sufficient. Three subscriptions therefore replaced what had been six by duplication. Back files were brought together, as were those of two other journals (one Italian, one German) which had ceased publication. Duplicates, about one-third of the total, were sold (this comes under the rubric: Burning your bridges behind you) for an appreciable sum, which was then available to perfect the five files which had been retained. Then four new subscriptions were begun, bringing to the area desired journals not previously available (Israeli, American, Polish, and Russian). With the revival of the supposedly dead Italian journal, there are now eight current journals where three had been before, but only one file of each instead of six files, half of which were duplicative. The total annual outlay has not increased by more than a few dollars.

This example fails to support convinc-ingly the claim for savings in ultimate book-storage capacity, though the reference to the elimination of duplicates suggests it. However, it is only necessary to think of closed serial entries, to appreciate how much can be gained by consolidating such files and disposing of all duplicates, where the nature of the material and of its use allows this. The situation and circumstances of each college library will determine for it what direction co-operation may most profitably take. The possible varieties are many. Independence and separation will inevitably bring their own train of difficulties for a college library. Contriving to make common cause with other libraries is a means of deferring, if not of avoiding, them. Such working together will be uninspiring and perfunctory if it is motivated solely by considerations of prudence, economy, or despair. As has already been suggested, it can and should be creative in intent, directed toward an improvement of resources.

Quality, to resume an earlier theme, has been a key word of much of this discussion. How do we know when we have it? The answers to this are tentative rather than final. All the attempts to appraise the quality of libraries have thus far cast no more than a limited amount of light. Waples candidly concluded, in his study for the North Central Association, that quality was defined operationally as "the number of titles on a prepared check list which the library has." Setting aside questions as to the appropriateness of such a list to a particular library and as to the essential quality of the list itself, this means that the results of such measuring are relative and not absolute. Surveys of individual libraries have employed check lists and comparative statistics with ingenuity and resourcefulness in an attempt to reach conclusions as to the adequacy or inadequacy of collections; yet they fall short of giving a conclusive statement concerning quality which can be used to guide us. Others have come at the matter indirectly by studies of how the books are acquired (book selection), or of how they are employed (use) or not employed (obsolescence). They have helped us all in heightening our awareness, in sharpening our perceptions, in enabling us to exercise more effectively the judgment and selection which lead toward quality. Yet book selection in which a large number of persons participate, as in a college, is not readily subject to control; studies of use, based on counting operations, are but poor reports of the infinitely complex relationship between a reader and his book; and obsolescence, which inevitably and falsely implies a correspondence between the age of a book and its increasing uselessness, leans dangerously and too heavily on formal evidence of loan, the least reliable record an open-stack library can have.

Here I become acutely aware that the announcement of this conference strongly implied that it was to be concerned with new problems and new approaches. There have been no startling revelations, no surprising flashes of insight, nor, to end suspense, are there likely to be. Eschewing the role of prophet, I can say but little to this point beyond what may have already been stated or implied. If in the future the college library is, as a matter of policy, to subtract as well as to add, there is good reason to ask whether a re-examination of its methods of cataloging, classifying, and record-keeping may not be in order. Libraries are always in danger of mistaking their means for their ends, but, more particularly, a commitment to flux rather than to permanent retention invites this

question: What can we do to make withdrawal less costly and less cumbersome? Though what was said of the Lamont Library *Catalogue* may have sounded slighting and severe, that was not intended as more than a comment on its usefulness as a description of the ideal contents of college libraries in general. Quite possibly, college libraries can usefully learn from it in the matter of the arranging and describing of books. To this same end a thoughtful perusal of Wyllis Wright's paper in the last issue of *College and Research Libraries* should be rewarding.[7]

Where duplicates for reserve use are concerned, the course to be followed is clear. They should be treated as a collection within the collection and given the minimum of processing, so that, as they fall into disuse, their discarding is made as easy as possible. With other books the solution cannot hope to be so clear and easy. This is a large subject, which can only be suggested. Furthermore, it is one which was specifically forsworn at the beginning.

And now, at the risk of repetition, let us cast a final glance at the present situation. Because the funds of private institutions are not infinitely elastic, fewer books are being acquired and the need for discriminating judgment in choosing them is correspondingly increased. The seemingly inevitable commitments to periodicals and continuations grow regularly more costly. This bespeaks their being subjected to the severest scrutiny and invokes the consideration of co-operation with other libraries where this is possible. Funds and costs are the upper and nether millstones ready to grind us small.

The effects of widespread research

7 W. E. Wright, "How Little Cataloging Can Be Effective?" *College and Research Libraries*, XV (April, 1954), 167–70, 175.

grants in the sciences, on their present scale a postwar phenomenon, pose another more particular type of problem. To support this work, highly specialized printed resources are often required. Too frequently the contracts for such grants are not written so as to allow for their purchase, with the consequence that heavy and unexpected costs fall upon the college library. This leads further, unless great care is taken, to a wide disparity between the extent and nature of the research resources supplied to the sciences and those for all the other disciplines. The humanities and the social sciences must be kept from becoming poor relations in the matter of library resources.

This implies a handsomeness of expenditure which ill accords with shrinking purchasing power. It is not an impossibility, however, if book funds are kept as free and fluid and manageable as possible. Under such conditions extemporizing is feasible, and the most effective utilization of available resources can be achieved.

A college library is the creature of its parent-institution. A very meager library would serve an indifferent faculty engaged in the perfunctory instruction of unwilling students. In all that has been said here it has been necessary to assume, on the contrary, a first-rate faculty of humane scholars, who do not mistake the scraps of learning for the feast, well trained, devoted to teaching, confronting capable students interested in learning.

"If you want your sons and brothers well taught," wrote Chauncey Tinker, "you must have teachers here who are men and learned men; if you are to keep learned men here, you must have a still and quiet place for them to read and think in; but, above all, you must have books for them—not merely a standard-ized fifty-thousand foot shelf, warranted sufficient for running a university, but a library of millions of volumes, with strange books in it, out of the way books, rare books and expensive books."[8] Cut down to size, this serves well to suggest the college library which is in my mind. Nor is this a figment of fancy. For unexplained reasons, women's colleges make handsomer provision for their libraries than do men's. Regard Vassar, Wellesley, Bryn Mawr, or Smith, to see the reality which my words only imply.

An anthology has been called an act of criticism. A college library is, on a large scale, an anthology. In the same way it involves and illustrates an attitude toward and a judgment on the various provinces of knowledge. Because it is the work of many hands over long periods of time, each college library develops as a distinct and highly individual anthology in this sense. Or, thinking of such a library as a collection, we may view it in terms of the private book collector, who is engaged in a stupid and unrewarding enterprise if he does no more than secure a printed bibliography to use as a buying list, but who finds it an exciting pursuit, a true act of creation, to see a subject, to obtain a mastery of it, and to illustrate it by his collecting. So the buying of a college library at any time deserves to be, not a slavish adherence to lists, approved, recommended, or best books, but the assembling of those materials appropriate to all the variable human and institutional elements present and acting at that time. And when they are gathered on the shelves, we must remember that it is not the books alone that matter. They are inert. It is what is done with them that counts in the end.

8 C. B. Tinker, "The University Library," *Yale Alumni Weekly*, XXXIII (February 29, 1924), 650.

THE COLLEGE-LIBRARY BUILDING

CHARLES M. ADAMS

T HE College-Library Building" in relation to "The Function of the Library in the Modern College" is certainly a title plain enough to call for no questioning as to meaning. A good craftsman can do creditable work without the latest tools, but he can do best work with good tools. A college librarian can do creditable work without a building of the latest style and plan, but he can do best work with a building well planned and skilfully designed for meeting the special needs of his college. So much, it seems to me, is the sum and substance of such a paper as this. We can, to be sure, look at the philosophy and trends of college-library architecture and the relation of the librarian to the architect, at new building materials and equipment, at varying ideas of arrangements, at changing needs of members of the faculty and students, and at operations and services of the library as they affect the building; we can do all that with profit. The battle cry of the Renaissance, however, should be repeated again and again: *Ars una; species mille.* The principle behind library planning, like the art of architecture, may be one; the examples have thousands of aspects. There is no single way to solve the problem of the library building.

The college-library building today is shaped around many of the topics which so far have been discussed at this conference. In some ways this conference may be considered as significant a contribution to the planning of a college-library building as the one which was held here eight years ago and devoted to the specific topic of library buildings. "Trends

and Developments in Undergraduate Education," "The Relation between the Library and Collegiate Objectives," and "The Nature of the Book Collection" are all topics as pertinent for a college-library building as are technical and administrative operations or as acoustical ceilings, rubber-tile floors, and modern air treatment. This statement is in no way intended to minimize the importance of making adequate provision for those library operations or to minimize the contribution which technology and new materials have made to the modern library building. It is nearly a century since Greenough and Sullivan put into words the age-old principle that "form follows function." That "a library building should be planned for library work" was the first point of agreement in 1891 among librarians as to library architecture.[1] William M. Randall at the 1946 institute said: "First study your needs for building in known functions to be fulfilled."[2] The principle of "functionalism"

---

[1] John E. Burchard, Charles W. David, and Julian P. Boyd (eds.), *Planning the University Library Building: A Summary of Discussions by Librarians, Architects, and Engineers* (Princeton: Princeton University Press, 1949). On p. 3 are listed nine of the still pertinent "Points of Agreement among Librarians as to Library Architect" originally published by Charles C. Soule in the *Library Journal* in 1891. This volume, based on a meeting of the Cooperative Committee on Library Building Plans, is a source for reference and study of the library. Although essentially concerned with the university library, it is pertinent for the college-library building as well.

[2] William M. Randall, "The Constitution of the Modern Library Building," in *Library Buildings for Library Service: Papers Presented before the Library Institute of the University of Chicago, August 5–10, 1946,* ed. Herman H. Fussler (Chicago: American Library Association, 1947).

expounded by librarians and architects has been the dominating influence on our library buildings. Now we have a conference on "The Functions of the Library in the Modern College." Out of these papers and discussions we should be able to plan and shape the library building of the modern college.

It was A. C. Cutter in 1888 who said that the architect is the natural enemy of the librarian.[3] As recently as 1952, Ralph Ellsworth wrote: "For over a century architects have had their way. Perhaps librarians can be forgiven for daring to assume a belligerent attitude."[4] Even in recent years there have been built far too many buildings on our campuses with little awareness of the library functions to be performed not to give some truth to these statements. As one looks back over the literature on library buildings, however, the contributions by architects stand out prominently. The boldness of Labrouste in planning stacks for the Bibliothèque Nationale in the 1860's and his use of an interior glass partition between the reading-room and stack areas needs only to be mentioned to recall a whole line of architects who have been alert to the working functions of libraries.[5] The success of the Cooperative Committee on Library Building Plans, established in 1944, was due as much to the participation of architects as to that of librarians.

The formal conferring on mutual problems by architects and librarians in recent years at institute meetings and on other occasions is a step forward in library planning. The tradition of conferences set by the Cooperative Committee has been carried on by the ACRL Library Buildings Committee in its annual institutes. The example of inviting architects, as well as administrators and building equipment engineers and manufacturers, has resulted in continued co-operation. The unco-operative architect today is about as rare as the untrained librarian. Robert Muller, in a recent review of Talbot Hamlin's *Forms and Functions of Twentieth-Century Architecture*, said that librarians reading these volumes "will rid themselves of the false notion that a librarian's idea of a library building must necessarily be in conflict with an architect's."[6] There may be easier and lighter ways of arriving at this understanding than plowing through these four volumes, but there are other good reasons for perusing these and similar studies in architecture. As librarians, it seems only just that we should understand some of the principles and practices of architecture, if we, in turn, expect the architect for the library to read and understand the functions and modern practices of librarianship.

The preparation of a written program stating the functions of the library in full is another forward step for a librarian in the planning of a library. Gerould emphasized this point in his book on *The College Library Building* in 1932. Mr. Gerould said:

Everyone has used libraries, of course, and, in a general way, knows what the building must contain. There must be reading rooms, stack

[3] "The Librarian and the Architect," in *Planning the University Library Building*, p. 138. The whole of chap. viii of this monograph is devoted to this topic and has much sound advice.

[4] Ralph E. Ellsworth, "Determining Factors in the Evaluation of the Modular Plan for Libraries," *College and Research Libraries*, XIV (April, 1953), 125–28, 142.

[5] Sigfried Giedion, *Space, Time, and Architecture: The Growth of a New Tradition* (3d. ed.; Cambridge: Harvard University Press, 1954); Helen Margaret Reynolds, "University Library Buildings in United States, 1890–1939," *College and Research Libraries*, XIV (April, 1953), 149–57, 166.

[6] *Forms and Functions of Twentieth-Century Architecture*, ed. Talbot F. Hamlin, reviewed by Robert H. Muller, *College and Research Libraries*, XV (April, 1954), 240–41.

rooms, an office for the librarian, a few rooms miscalled "seminars," and possibly, if one is very modern, a browsing room; but the dimension of these rooms, and their relation each to the other, is seldom given proper study. A few notes, together with the limit of cost, are turned over to the architect; and he is expected to produce a proper building.[7]

Since Gerould's time, and due in part to his sound analytical study of the college library, the written program for a library building has received continued emphasis. How to draft the program and exactly what it should contain are still in the early stages of development. Ernest J. Reece has recently devoted a thorough study to programs, their values and how to draft them, which has been published in *College and Research Libraries*.[8] The program has grown out of the principle of functionalism in architecture and is welcomed by the architect. In fact, there have been occasions when no program was provided by the librarian or the college and the architect has proceeded to have one prepared. As the four-line staff with single notation has been developed by the composer into full orchestration for the musicians, so the program is fast becoming a score with equal potentialities for the librarian. Or, to make the analogy more direct, the program as an instrument of planning may become as significant for the librarian as he turns to the architect for performance, as the blueprint is for the architect as he turns over his work to the builder. The fact that it may not have the exactness of the blueprint (or musical notation) does not lessen the influence which it has as a guide for the architect, who can no longer

be expected, in the rush and complexity of our society—even of that in our college communities—to grasp fully and to analyze the library functions of any particular institution. Here is the challenge to the librarian which will require the whole of his training in librarianship, a knowledge of his institution, and a creative ability to express the functions of his institution in terms significant to his architect.

The program is more than a project to sell the library building to the administration or to help raise a million dollars. The program should set forth the objectives of the library in relation to the teaching program and in terms of student and faculty needs for a library, as well as in details of operations, flow of workbook capacities, and air-conditioning. The key to its success may lie in understanding the institution, on the one hand, and architecture, on the other. As definitely and as simply as possible the librarian must express the purposes and functions of his particular library. He may be aided by figures and charts. Most agree that he should not attempt to draw actual arrangements or design. The style of architecture, however, is a matter for which preference may be indicated. In fact, the program may be used as the basis for selection of the architect trained in a particular style. It is recognized that the so-called "modern" architecture has become a style as pronounced, as defined, as any other style, with all the restrictions, disciplines, limitations, and blessings that we associate with the term.[9] Under these circumstances "the program" becomes essential to an institution which wishes to be assured of a functioning library rather than a period piece.

[7] James Thayer Gerould, *The College Library Building: Its Planning and Equipment* (New York: Charles Scribner's Sons, 1932), p. 15.

[8] Ernest J. Reece, "Library Building Programs: How To Draft Them," *College and Research Libraries*, XIII (July, 1952), 198–211.

[9] Matthew Nowicki, "Origins and Trends in Modern Architecture," *Magazine of Art*, XLVI (November, 1951), 273–79.

In recent years a number of people, because of interest and experience in library building, have become experts, serving as consultants: library consultants, architect consultants, engineer equipment consultants, and professional planners. These men and women have a valuable role to play in the planning of a library building. Not all of us have the opportunity to plan a building or the aptitude to think in terms of spaces or blueprints. It may be that the librarian is living almost too close to his own problems. A survey by an outsider may help formulate the functions of a particular library with a clarity that the librarian at home often cannot command. A consultant may save him from many a false start and, as the program and planning develop, prove a real economy to an institution. Consultants have learned through their own errors and successes as well as through those of others. However, they must be selected with as much care as the architect. Neutra, in his new study *Survival through Design*, devotes a chapter to consultants which he heads in explanation as follows: "The 'vested' expert—'witty' or just sour—rises against innovation more often than the common man. On the other side, innovators frequently have one-track minds and cannot comprehend all the doings of their own brain children."[10]

The librarian can visit new library buildings and can read descriptive plans and programs of many others. The value of these to the librarian is as real as the use of consultants, but using new buildings as authority also has its dangers. Attendance at institutes where existing library buildings are criticized for their failures and successes and where new plans are presented for evaluation has many advantages. At these meetings a librarian is helped to think in terms of space relations, architectural styles, and materials, and to look at a plan or a blueprint more intelligently. By such visits and attendance at conferences a librarian can learn about consultants and architects and have the opportunity to discuss his own problems with his colleagues.

The descriptive articles on new college libraries,[11] along with some analytical literature on library buildings,[12] give one some down-to-earth views of accomplishments and trends in the college-library field. Almost all the articles on new buildings have mentioned the favorable site which was obtained for the library. This usually was as centrally located as possible, on established lines of student traffic, or on lines contemplated for the future development of the college. Some allowance was usually given for possible expansion, and the description often indicated whether this was to be vertical or horizontal. The architect had in some cases actually made plans for such ex-

---

[10] Richard Neutra, *Survival through Design* (New York: Oxford University Press, 1954). The book contains a number of interesting and stimulating observations; thus: "Functionalism can turn into a superficial creed for extroverts, but it can also be guided to honor the functions within our skin and the innermost life"; "Function may itself be a follower" (chap. xv); "Design, never a harmless play with forms and colors, changes outer life as well as our inner balances" (chap. xliv).

[11] Edna Hanley Byers (comp.), "A College and University Library Buildings Bibliography, 1945–1953," in *ACRL Monograph*, No. 10 (1953), pp. 81–98. Mrs. Byers is bringing this bibliography up to date in the forthcoming issue of the *ACRL Monograph* devoted to the proceedings of the 1954 ACRL Buildings Plans Institute held at Madison, Wisconsin.

[12] Ernest J. Reece, "Building Planning and Equipment," *Library Trends*, I (July, 1952), 136–55 (with bibliography). For building trends see also Robert H. Muller, "Future Library Building Trends among Colleges and Universities," *College and Research Libraries*, XII (January, 1951), 33–36; and J. F. Vanderheyden, "Contemporary Building Planning as It Appears to a European Librarian," *College and Research Libraries*, X (October, 1949), 367–78.

pansion, erecting only the first unit of a much larger building. The entrance was usually at street or ground level or with but a few steps. There was one public entrance or, at most, two. The old monumentality, or "heroism," of many former libraries seemed completely absent. This did not mean that the buildings were without dignity and attractiveness. The efficiency of the "warehouse" with its almost perfect "functionalism" had made few gains on the college campus. Problems of landscaping and even of parking were considered. More often than not the library conformed in style of architecture with other buildings of the campus rather than striking out in bold new lines. Even those buildings which were frankly modern in style seemed to make subtle reference in materials or lines to neighboring older buildings. Except for the fact that some buildings were labeled "The Library" and were centrally located and new, it would be necessary still for a visitor to inquire for the library. The building had acquired no especially uniform features or characteristics which its functions gave to its design. In fact, the variety of fronts, entrances, lines, and treatments has shown a healthy refusal to copy the designs of other colleges. Although several descriptions of new libraries apologized, so to speak, for the traditional style—or defended their modern lines—few failed to emphasize the successful planning and arrangement of the interiors. Most librarians expressed real satisfaction in what had been accomplished for the successful operation of library activities through their buildings.

The key word in most of the planning today is "flexibility." It has become almost synonymous with "functionalism." Flexibility usually refers to the ability to make major changes in the building arrangement. "Adaptability" is the word used to refer usually to the ability to make minor changes in arrangement of furniture and equipment. "Expansibility" is another element which is characteristic of flexibility. The problem for the librarian is to determine as nearly as possible the functions which are most likely to be changed in a building over a period of years or, possibly, seasonally. For example, during the regular terms the student body may number a thousand or so undergraduates; but during the summer months the enrolment may drop to four or five hundred or jump to three thousand, and use of the library may be much more in the pattern required for conferences and institutes. The building should be adaptable to any such changes and the resulting necessary economies. It may be necessary to build only a part of a projected total building, allowing for growing book collections and increased enrolment. The greatest need for flexibility lies in the relation of the teaching program to the library. The changes here result from the introduction of new schools and departments or shifts to new programs. Some consultants in "general education" have estimated an increase in library use of as much as four or five times in the institutions which have made the change from the traditional liberal arts curriculum. For some the "modular" type of construction seems to answer many of the requirements for flexibility demanded by our libraries. Although in architecture the module is among the most restrictive of forms, as a building principle it has been successfully used in Georgian, French Provincial, and Collegiate Gothic, as well as in "Modern." It lends itself to the development of our "open" arrangements of books and readers, emphasizing the horizontal development of interiors. It appears to have economies especially where the needs of readers have become of equal importance with the book collections, or even greater. The danger may come as a unit size is developed which is economical for shelving books, efficient for chair and table arrangements, and yet fails to meet space requirements for readers. As each module tends to become adaptable for all functions, including those new requirements for audio-visual materials and economical storage areas, the cost per unit may become too high and the function for any one purpose never be adequately fulfilled. The crystallizing and resulting standardization of the module may be its own death. Modular planning, however, is an exciting development which may remove certain rigidity from interior arrangements and, used with modification, give some flexibility rather than "exactitude" to library areas. Many college libraries have used this type of construction, and it has many enthusiastic supporters. It is well worth visiting several of the buildings which have used this technique, to obtain some idea of its possibilities and its weaknesses. In recent years it has received very careful analytical study.[13] Flexibility, it must be remembered, may be obtained in various ways in architecture, and "modular" construction does not necessarily guarantee flexibility for all functions.

Management engineers have contributed much to the efficiency of our buildings and have made careful studies from which many good standards have been developed.[14] Costs are being analyzed in square feet of space available for library functions rather than in cubic feet of a building. Lines of traffic, controls, location of offices, stairs, elevators, book storage, ventilation, maintenance, lighting, and a whole list of other details have received and are continuing to receive careful study. There is little excuse for those with a new building to have inefficient or poor operational facilities. New materials, such as glass, acoustical tile, cinder blocks, and rubber-tile floors, have been used with success in the improvement of buildings. Obsolescence of many of our college libraries has been due as much to improper study of relations of areas and offices as to lack of space for books and readers.

The interior of the college-library building has become more "open" in recent years not only physically but also in relation to readers' use of material and their freedom to move about. Controls and services have been centralized, usually by an entrance, and, instead of rooms, there are areas which tend to be without exact limits as they flow into each other. Most stacks, if there are stacks in the old sense at all, are of open access, although in a few descriptions of new buildings it is timidly implied that these stacks can be closed if necessary. More often stacks and reading areas are together, with no permanent physical barriers of any kind between the books and the readers. The arrangement, although open for the libraries, tends to retain central areas for reference, circula-

[13] Ralph E. Ellsworth, "Determining Factors in the Evaluation of the Modular Plan for Libraries," *College and Research Libraries*, XIV (April, 1953), 125–28, 142. Angus MacDonald has promised, I understand, a monograph on this subject. A check through *Library Literature* will turn up a number of other studies on modular construction.

[14] Angus MacDonald, "Building Design for Library Management," *Library Trends*, II (January, 1954), 463–69. Some other recent articles on management are: Donald Coney, "Management in College and University Libraries," *Library Trends*, I (July, 1952), 74–83 (with bibliography); and Maurice F. Tauber, T. D. Morris, and Robert E. Kingery, "Management Improvements in Libraries," *College and Research Libraries*, XV (April, 1954), 188–204; see also Keyes D. Metcalf, "Spatial Problems in University Libraries," *Library Trends*, II (April, 1954), 554–61.

tion, serials, order, and cataloging, in the traditional pattern for operations. This includes an area for reserve. A few have dared to put the reserves along with each subject field throughout the library; but, on the whole, the reserve-room, or its equivalent, is still present in most of the new college libraries, despite the lamentations of some librarians.[15]

A variation of the "open" development is to divide the library into three or more large subject divisions or areas of knowledge.[16] Each of these, such as the humanities, the social sciences, or the natural sciences, has its own open arrangement for reference, periodicals, reserves, and stacks, with a subject-trained librarian in charge. This development seems particularly successful for the medium-sized university, where much emphasis is given to the undergraduate teaching program, and the practice has grown especially in the Middle and Far West. The divisional type of arrangement, although used in part by a few small college libraries, has not become popular among the liberal arts colleges. The subject departmental arrangement in rooms has practically disappeared, except where a location may call for a service outside the main building. New build-

ings offer many colleges the opportunity to centralize scattered collections and departmental libraries. Except for a few dormitory, laboratory, or memorial collections, centralization has won approval on most college campuses. Not only is it efficient from a management point of view, but the gathering of all fields of knowledge into one working collection has value as a teaching instrument in the liberal arts or general education of students.

More consideration for the undergraduates' library needs is now given by the larger universities in their new buildings.[17] Most have set aside at least a single large room and have provided space for a staff to service undergraduates and develop collections of special interest to them. The most significant recognition seems to be in providing a completely separate building developed from a program of careful study of the problems of the undergraduates in the university and the awareness of their needs as distinguished from those of the graduate and research students.

Teaching with books, the laboratory workshop, the library as a teaching instrument, and the library in college instruction are all ideas as well as titles of publications, which have been influential in the planning of buildings.[18] The integration between library operations and

[15] William R. Lansberg, "Current Trends in College Reserve Room," *College and Research Libraries*, XI (April, 1950), 120–24, 136.

[16] There are many articles on "divisional" libraries, a few of which are: Patricia Marvin, "Circulation in the Divisional Library: The New Plan of Service," *College and Research Libraries*, XII (July, 1951), 241–44, 265; Percy D. Morrison, "Variation of the Subject Divisional Plan at Oregon," *College and Research Libraries*, XIV (April, 1953), 158–63; J. R. Blanchard, "Departmental Libraries in Divisional Plan University Libraries," *College and Research Libraries*, XIV (July, 1953), 243–48 (see bibliography, p. 248); John D. Chapman, Ralph H. Hopp, and Arthur J. Vernix, "The Divisional Library at Nebraska: Two Aspects," *College and Research Libraries*, XV (April, 1954), 148–57.

[17] Arthur M. McAnally, Stanley E. Gwynn, Philip J. McNiff, William S. Dix, and Wyman S. Parker, "Library Service to Undergraduates: A Symposium," *College and Research Libraries*, XIV (July, 1953), 266–75.

[18] Harvie Branscomb, *Teaching with Books* (Chicago: Association of American Colleges and American Library Association, 1940); Committee on the New Library, *A Laboratory-Workshop Library for Princeton* (Princeton: The Committee, 1944); University Library Planning Committee, *The Library as a Teaching Instrument* (Iowa City: The Committee, 1945); Louis R. Wilson *et al.*, *The Library in College Instruction* (New York: H. W. Wilson Co., 1951).

the teaching program has become an objective.[19] It may be easier to talk of these principles than to translate them into blueprints. Also it seems easier to criticize blueprints from the point of view of management than of academic objectives. It is necessary, however, to look critically at plans to see whether the general principles sought by librarians are actually incorporated in the building. It may be scanned in two ways: from the point of view of members of the faculty and from that of the student.

An awareness of faculty needs has been expressed in a number of ways. Faculty studies are now a part of most college-library buildings, just as they are accepted in the university. There is hardly a new college library that does not provide some conference, seminar, or, to be more accurate, classroom space for those faculty members who find teaching with books in the library a stimulating experience. Some colleges are providing lounges for faculty as well as for the staff within the library. There may be hope that some of the faculty members may wish to work there for as many hours as does the library staff. At any rate, members of the faculty are now welcomed with facilities which have been especially planned for them.

The library collection itself has become more useful for faculty research needs. Microfilm, photostat, microphotography, photoreproductions, and other developments have made it possible for the scholar now to conduct much of his work in the limited collection of the college library. The development of interlibrary loan and tools for bibliographical control within the means of a college library has tended to bring the college professor into the library. He no longer needs a holiday or vacation to get the opportunity to dash to a metropolitan or university collection.

Another development in faculty-library relations is the status of the library staff.[20] In most of our buildings there is little question of the administrative importance of the librarian. His office is usually furnished with all the requisites of an executive. I know of one college librarian who did not want such an office for himself but was overruled. He now has a most beautiful office; but, I understand, seldom uses it except to show to visitors. He did not wish to work in the isolation of an executive. As the library staff takes its position alongside the teaching faculty, the new buildings are recognizing the academic functions of the librarian as distinct from administrative or from clerical and semiprofessional, so-called "housekeeping," operations. Members of college faculties are human, in often failing to see anything but clerical routines or administrative duties in library work. If I remember correctly, one library deliberately provided a glass wall for the office of each librarian, so that faculty members could see the librarians actually working with books just as they themselves might do. Desks are replacing counters in public areas, and adequate office space for cataloging, bibliography, and book selecting on the part of the library staff is being provided. In some instances the space is the envy of "classroom" faculty members, who sometimes wistfully recall that they once had thought of becoming librarians!

A number of developments have sharpened the librarian's awareness and ability to control problems of the ever

[19] W. L. Williamson, "Relating the Library to the Classroom: Some Specific Suggestions," *College and Research Libraries*, XIV (April, 1953), 167–71.

[20] Frank A. Lundy, "Faculty Rank of Professional Librarians," *College and Research Libraries*, XII (January, April, 1951), 11–19, 109–22.

increasing size of the book collection.[21] Weeding the collection of little-used materials and actual removal of dead wood is now an established practice. The college library is no longer fearful of unlimited growth. It may now give up many things which its faculty would never have permitted ten or twenty years ago. Economical areas for storage and for compact shelving now make possible the holding of materials for a period to test their usefulness without sacrificing the openness and freedom of the general collections. The co-operative development of economical storage areas for a community or region is helping the college library to meet many of the specialized demands of faculty or honor students and to free space for undergraduate needs.

The most striking recognition of readers in the new libraries is the care and taste with which the building is now furnished. A generous use of color in all shades has become a common practice. We read of such colors as "Silver Birch," "Royal Violet," "Yellow Leaf," "Byzantine Blue," "Bittersweet," "Dew Mixture," "Pinkie," and slate gray or "Thunderbolt."[22] The students like these new colors, and some faculty members give approval. The furniture is carefully selected for comfort. Even in reserve-rooms there are occasional pieces inviting informality and suitable for long periods of reading. The arrangement has been considered for its attractiveness as well as for

[21] Blanche P. McCrum, Helmer Webb, and Rutherford D. Rogers, "Optimum Size of Libraries: A Symposium," *College and Research Libraries*, XI (April, 1950), 137–50.

[22] These colors have been quoted from Price Gilbert Library, Georgia Institute of Technology, *Dedication Program*, November 21, 1953, Atlanta, Georgia. Many other striking and original colors and combinations are referred to frequently in articles on new library buildings for colleges as well as universities.

its efficiency. Green plants, framed pictures, and window draperies are part of the decoration. The librarian, with the help of the library equipment houses, has given beauty and smartness, as well as utility, to the furnishings. An institutional designer has been consulted for a number of new buildings. Some architects have accepted this responsibility early in the planning stage, recognizing that the success of a new building will depend as much on the interior furnishings as on the design and style of the building. There have been some studies on the relation between environment and work in libraries which may give more than just artistic reasons for use of color, quiet floors, translucent or clear partitions, and lighting arrangements.

From the point of view of the students, it has been recognized that too large collections, such as those in many of the major universities, can actually be a handicap to undergraduates. The college library no longer wants its shelves filled with little-used or obsolescent materials. Moreover, with "open" arrangement, these somewhat "dead" materials become very conspicuous and are usually not too attractive to undergraduates as they are encouraged to work among the collections. College libraries are becoming larger, but the emphasis is directed more to the working needs of students in use of library materials rather than to ever increasing collections which crowd out the reader. The percentage of the student body to be served at any one time has been increased. Students are also provided with carrels, typing areas, "talking" or group working-rooms, smoking privileges, and other amenities. Frank Lloyd Wright, in speaking of public library buildings recently, said that they should be "unpretentious in human scale, designed for comfort and enjoyment of people who love books—a happy place with music and a pleasant home-likeness."[23] Man as a physiological measure in architecture has been receiving continued emphasis.

Since the library has freed its books from medieval chains, it has learned to handle many new media and other forms of communications. Some of the functions of these new media are to be discussed later at this conference. Although the library may not be designated as the "Communications Center" for the college, it is often able to help with uses of new materials for teaching, such as music and language disks, films and film strips, tapes, as well as maps, prints, and other audio-visual teaching aids. Some libraries have admitted what is called the "living" book, by providing areas for lectures and group programs. This may be following the footsteps of the public libraries and their branches in providing such services for the community. All such programs offer a number of problems in library administration.

The library in the modern college is accepting slowly the need for additional areas for students and faculty who wish to work in groups with many new media of communications, as well as for space for the individual to work in quiet with a single volume. The small lecture hall or auditorium has appeared in many college libraries. It is often associated with areas for projecting films and a center for photoelectric communication equipment. How educational television is to be brought into the college library is still a question, but I should not be surprised to see some college libraries already providing space for this. I only hope that translating machines will not get so small or

cheap that the library will be asked to plug some of these into the shelf for the foreign-language dictionaries!

There is another area of activity which is becoming more important to the college library and for which college buildings are providing space. This is in the field of exhibitions, public relations, and publications. The strategic location of the library gives it an opportunity to operate an exhibition program which can have real value for the library and community. A separate gallery on an upper floor by a special collection is not the usual treatment and is seldom found in the college library. Space for this activity is right up in front and located at points of heavy traffic. In fact, by the use of glass the whole front is sometimes used to advantage for a continual live exhibit of the whole library, or an attractive part of it, in action for all who pass by. Unfortunately, most exhibition equipment is rather formal and heavy or built into corridors or walls so as to be rigid and not easily adaptable to changing programs of varying size. The exhibition areas are like the Procrustean bed in which each victim is killed because it is too large or too small. Moreover, most exhibition equipment is too expensive. The college library needs to control its materials, but it does not specialize in illuminated manuscripts, incunabula, or other rarities requiring the dignity or security of heavy bronze cases. George Nelson, in the comments and Introduction to his new book *Display*, has some ideas which are quite applicable to college libraries.[24] With ex-

[23] S. Janice Kee, "Let's Have Good Libraries, Not Big Ones, Says Frank Lloyd Wright," *ALA Bulletin*, XLVI (October, 1952), 293.

[24] George Nelson (ed.), *Display* (New York: Whitney Publications, 1953). The following introductory note seems pertinent: "It is not easy to express these feelings in permanent buildings today: there is the conservation of owners, of building codes, of the FHA, of banks, of trade unions. But in temporary exposition—why not? The need to be practical does not exist, the necessity to build inexpensively does. The designer can ease up a bit and

hibitions one is not tied down to a conservative long-term building style, but one does have a problem of expense. In exhibition areas one can afford to experiment with space and to use more temporary equipment with virtues of adaptability and expansibility.

Along with exhibitions should go an area for preparation of these exhibits. It will save much of the staff time and make it possible to use others in this work without upsetting one's office. The exhibitions often call for publicity; this leads into the related areas of special services. There should be space for preparation of booklets, handbooks, annual reports, and other publications which the college library can issue with profit. Instruction in library use has its program, for which the lecture hall, a leaflet on library use, and tours are all important. Do not forget, when you get that new library building, that you will have many visitors for years. There were plenty even in the old building. Some have a space to sit and visit. "Meet me at the library" should not be discouraged.

William Warner Bishop, in his paper on "The Historical Development of Library Buildings" at the Graduate Library School Conference of 1946, concluded with a section on "American Trends." "The model," he said, "is frankly the modern department store."[25] Many of those predicted influences may now be seen. The library is given a location right on lines of traffic, and readers are entering directly at street level. The libraries' "wares" are housed in the "open" manner and are attractively displayed. Although restraint is present, the trend may still be, as one of our colleagues said, "with appearance as modern as the best store in town,"[26] or, as an architect put it, "form follows sale."

The question raised by Wyllis Wright in his recent paper, "How Little Cataloging Can Be Effective?"[27] is characteristic of many other shifts in emphasis. It may be that we are becoming more complicated in our functions; but it is heartening to note that in some areas the process is quite the reverse. As the college library accepts additional responsibility for new media of communication, community services, open shelves, and bibliographical control, it may at the same time evaluate and simplify its book resources, its storage responsibilities, its cataloging, and its circulation procedures in such ways as to compensate for added functions. I predict only that the college library will survive.

The librarian may well wonder, as did Mr. Fussler in 1946 in his Introduction to the published proceedings of that conference, "whether our imperfect buildings do not grow in part out of our imperfect knowledge of what goes on within libraries."[28] The librarian today has been given a key position in the partnership of planning his building. The answer to the question of what constitutes a good library building may come from the li-

---

enjoy himself. The result can be fun. It is surprising how often it is significant fun." He illustrates and comments on a number of trends in modern book-display work. It is simply described as "a cage within a shell" in which modern Italian designers are now at the top of the field.

[25] William Warner Bishop, "The Historic Development of Library Buildings," in *Library Buildings for Library Service*. The section on "American Trends" occurs on pp. 10–11.

[26] Ralph E. Ellsworth, "Appearance as Modern as the Best Store in Town," *Library Journal*, LXXIV (December 15, 1949), 1851.

[27] Wyllis E. Wright, "How Little Cataloging Can Be Effective?" *College and Research Libraries* XV (April, 1954), 167–70, 175.

[28] Herman H. Fussler, "Introduction," *Library Buildings for Library Service*, p. vi.

brarian's knowledge of what goes on within and without the walls of his own library. This implies more than ever before a knowledge and appreciation of books. It also includes the ability to understand the needs of the college community as a whole and of the individuals struggling to learn and to communicate the best which has survived in society.

Although the college librarian with a new building to plan has many a headache (and heartache) in store for him, he also has a much envied opportunity of providing a resource which, in the long run, will improve the quality of work that goes on inside the building and out from it to members of the faculty and the student body.

COLLEGE-LIBRARY PERSONNEL

WYMAN W. PARKER

VARIOUS voices have been raised in the last decades calling for a philosophy of librarianship. Any agreement in the past has been limited to a description of general social usefulness, but these pacts have been so fragmentary and dubious that they inspired no confidence in the profession. Certainly, we ought to be able to formulate something more contemporary and more exact than the admirable original statement that attended the founding of the A.L.A. in 1876; that was to promote "the library interests of the country, and of increasing reciprocity of intelligence and goodwill among librarians and all interested in library economy and bibliographical studies."[1] Metcalf, Russell and Osborn, spokesmen of our library era, deplore the lack of any theoretical discussion to serve as the foundation of librarianship. College librarians, who are certainly equipped to deal with such analysis, ought to be even more concerned to outline at least a *modus vivendi* until the ideal is formulated.

From the vast and largely uninspiring quagmire of wrangling about education for librarianship, strong statements emerge, indicating a trend in thinking about the qualifications of the college librarian. The triumvirate just mentioned deplore the undue emphasis on technical routines for librarians; Professor Reece calls for more knowledge of books rather than of techniques for the college worker; and Dean White

quests for bookmen rather than technicians. In his wise and readable book, *Teaching with Books*, Harvie Branscomb makes no bones about the mistake that librarianship for colleges has made in "emphasizing routines and techniques rather than intellectual interests and educational insight."[2]

Factually, we have statistics to counter these none too delicate inferences that all is not well in the field of college-library personnel. Statistics tell us that we have some 6,000 College Libraries Section members of A.C.R.L., but they do not tell us how successfully these librarians are doing the essential job. Statistics told us that the colleges needed fifteen hundred library-school graduates after the war; but we know that this demand has not been met and that it cannot be completely satisfied by the number and types of library-school graduates currently available. Anyway, I distrust statistics, as they tend to indulge the librarian's reliance on mechanical aids, for, like a crutch, they only prop up existing weaknesses. Statistics present no moral incentives, and they fail to differentiate in quality. Besides the fact that they can be manipulated or made to lie, they offer no wisdom or humor. For example, a University of Cincinnati professor needed no impressive array of statistics to rout a long faculty discussion on inverting the M.A. He merely asked, if the degree were designated A.M., whether the faculty would

---

[1] C. S. Thompson, *Evolution of the American Public Library, 1653-1876* (Washington: Scarecrow Press, 1952), p. 219.

[2] Harvie Branscomb, *Teaching with Books* (Chicago: Association of American Colleges and the American Library Association, 1940), p. 86.

be logical and award an S.B. Kinsey need not have gone to the trouble of compiling his second report on sexual habits, had he heeded Ovid:

For girls as well as men enjoy
The sweets we steal from Venus' store.[3]

The place of the library in the college has been well covered by Professor Arragon. There is no need to reiterate that the college library's chief function is to serve the educational objectives of that college, to aid the faculty in its work, and to assist the students in their courses. As a service agency to special scholarship, the college library has objectives that are usually bounded by the ideals of the particular college. College-library collections are surely more limited than those of the research library, whose primary responsibility is to preserve knowledge, no matter how ephemeral the interpretation or how ancient the inquiry. College collections likewise tend to be less various and more scholarly than those of the average public library. The college library ought to serve impartially all the disciplines of its institution, while the librarian gains strength in campus councils by representing no departmental interest. Naturally, each college has its strong fields, and the good librarian must take proper cognizance of them. In fact, it is the librarian's duty to see that the college capitalizes on unusual collections and offers those courses that can appropriately take advantage of a wealth of material. Oberlin's good use of its comprehensive collection of Spanish drama is a case in point. When a considerable collection of books and prints of ethnological value was given to another Ohio college, it was its librarian's responsibility to urge the

offering of courses in anthropology. Thus the librarian serves the ideals of the college, which in the end means serving the faculty, for there is found the major concern for educational standards. Abbé Cotton des Houssayes in the eighteenth century recognized this when he spoke before the faculty as the newly appointed librarian of the Sorbonne: "I venture to hope that your kindness will sustain my weakness; I shall have to support me your counsels, which I shall ever make it a duty to follow. Your spirit, your hands even, I am fain to believe, will aid me in arranging, in ornamenting, in maintaining, in enlarging your library."[4]

The librarian in the college is more of a teacher than the university librarian, for example, whose concern is more with administration, organization, and bibliography. Branscomb epitomizes the main qualifications for a librarian in the college as follows: (a) a knowledge of the principles of library administration; (b) scholarly interests and understanding, including an interest in education on the undergraduate level; and (c) ability to work with students and to co-operate with the faculty.

Fortunately, college presidents now realize that the librarian must have faculty rank, thus granting official sanction to his campus standing. In recent years the college librarian is more often appointed full professor or even dean in the larger institutions. Regardless of the rank bestowed upon the college librarian, the individual has to earn the esteem of the faculty. There is but one standard in the college, and that, the academic. Administrative officers may be excused as instructed agents when they hand out varying appropriations, but the professor wants to understand the librarian's

[3] Ovid, . . . Ars amatoria . . . , trans. F. A. Wright (London: Routledge, 1925), p. 126.

[4] Philobiblion, VII (March, 1863), 55.

educational motives before taking grace-
fully the librarian's refusal to underwrite some pet departmental project.

Randall's statement in 1932 still
holds true: "The college librarian cannot hope for faculty standing and faculty privileges until he is willing to be
judged by faculty standards."[5] Randall
then warned the profession not to insist
upon faculty rank until librarians deserve it in accordance with academic
criteria. There are, indeed, a few in our
ranks with reservations concerning the
safety of books intrusted to the librarian's care. The late Randolph G. Adams
had his doubts cogently expressed in two
charming essays: "Librarians as Ene-
mies of Books" and "How Shall I Leave
My Books to a Library?"[6]

There is, in the conventional phrase,
"a wealth of literature" about the librarian as a teacher. It is surely more exact
to say that our index, *Library Literature*,
lists an enormous amount of print on the
controversy about whether a librarian
should teach, and if so, how much. It
ranges in these last decades from the
position of Glenn Brown, who feels that
the librarian has a job of his own in organizing and preserving the written and
printed record. He would not allow the
librarian to become entangled in the
teacher's responsibility, which he terms
"elucidation." The librarian's problem,
he states, is one of presentation. There
are some who might argue that the selection required in any presentation represents an elucidation or reflects a bias.
The other extreme is taken by Dean B.
Lamar Johnson in *The Librarian and the
Teacher in General Education* . . . (Chicago: American Library Association,

[5] W. M. Randall, *The College Library* (Chicago:
American Library Association and University of
Chicago Press, 1932), p. 59.

[6] *Library Quarterly*, VII (July, 1937), 317–31;
New Colophon, III (October, 1950), 146–52.

1948). He places the classroom within
the library, thereby as fully involving
the librarian in teaching a discipline as
in administering the books. There are
notable examples of librarians who are
as well known for their teaching activities as for their efforts in behalf of the
library. This conference has been fortunate in hearing one of the very best,
Newton McKeon. Alexander Laing, of
Dartmouth, Dr. Philip Benjamin, of
Allegheny, and Dr. Evelyn Little, of
Mills, are a few of the many others.

It might be fruitful to discover what
the college president, as ultimate authority within the college, looks for in a librarian. When Dr. McAfee was president
of Wellesley, she was fortunate in having
Miss Blanche McCrum as the Wellesley
librarian. President McAfee therefore
speaks from fine experience in maintaining that the college librarian "must encourage students, faculty and undergraduate, to handle their tools as effectively as possible. He is apt to do this
best by being himself a workman who
enjoys working with books, but he needs
more than a fondness for books. He
needs the art of spreading his enthusiasm to other workers."[7] She goes on to
say that the librarian's task is to educate his associates so that they will further his policies for library development.
President McEwen, of Hamilton, a former librarian, points out that the dominant area of activity in the library is
academic, as it is in the college, and that
the shared interest of the faculty in
teaching and research gives a sense of
security to those belonging to the group.
"Any complete acceptance of college
librarians as full colleagues," he says,
"must therefore await proof that the
librarians are genuine participants in

[7] *College and Research Libraries*, II (September,
1941), 302.

these shared interests."[8] He expects that every college librarian ought to be deeply and genuinely interested in some subject field and that this interest will gain the approbation of the librarian's faculty colleagues, regardless of whether or not his research gains recognition abroad.

Chancellor Branscomb, of Vanderbilt, does not go so far, although he gladly accepts as profit any special knowledge the librarian may have. He demands as essential qualifications of the librarian an understanding of research methods, a wide general knowledge, and an interest in educational procedures and results. Given these qualities, "further mastery of a special field of study can only be regarded as an additional asset, which will aid the librarian in many ways and enrich the intellectual life of the community."[9] This position reminds him of the oft quoted paternal advice, "Never marry a girl, my son, because she has money; but if she happens to have some, don't hold that against her." Branscomb notes that, although teaching adds to the librarian's stature in the eyes of colleagues as proof of his understanding of academic problems, it does result in divided allegiance. Therefore, special care must be taken to see that the librarian spends an adequate proportion of time on service to his patrons. Any teaching, Branscomb believes, ought to be clearly subordinate to the librarian's principal job, but, where the duties of the library permit, "some teaching may be a useful and helpful experience, particularly if it utilizes and keeps alive some special intellectual interest."[10]

We are all concerned to find such paragons to continue this fine and, in some cases, fictional tradition of bookmen-librarians. Much has been written about recruiting for the profession in this postwar era, but no one has promulgated a plan to end the striving. Of course, there should be no end to it, for we will always want better librarians and will always yearn to attract the very best to the profession. The library schools are the immediate source of trained personnel, and they perform commendable service in giving a uniform course of essential special facts. They utilize the usual devices in recruitment, such as publicity, interviews, scholarships, talks, and, above all, the reputation of a good curriculum served by competent authorities. But the responsibility for securing the most desirable candidates does not end with the library school. It cannot reach out much further without entering promotional schemes that are distasteful to the normal reserve of the librarian. A broadcast campaign may be very fruitful for enlistments to the Navy, the Marine Corps, and the Army, but such touting for librarians could only result in a disastrous lowering of the present level, and discontent would abound. There is definite need to look beyond the library schools for good library recruits. Surely librarians in both public and institutional work are aware of their obligation to watch for and foster those individuals that have a particular curiosity about books and libraries. Certain libraries have a fine reputation as a continuous source of supply to our professional schools. Colleges likewise put many students on the path to library school, usually through the joint agency of the department of English and the library staff.

It is important to discern certain characteristics in choosing candidates for college-library work. Of decided value

[8] *Ibid.*, III (June, 1942), 260.

[9] Branscomb, *op. cit.*, p. 91.

[10] *Ibid.*, p. 100.

is a broad cultural background, showing a curious and adaptable mind; for it is unfortunately true that the broader aspects of education cannot be accommodated in the professional curriculum. In these days, when it is comparatively easy to secure a well-paid position in industry, more importance should be attached to a special interest in books. Lawrence Powell goes to the very hub when he calls: "Give us librarians who have an overwhelming passion for books, who are bookmen by birth and by choice, by education, profession, and hobby. Properly channeled and directed, this passion for books is the greatest single basic asset a librarian can have."[11] In the past we have sinned by courting the technician, but certainly management engineering gives greater rewards both in salary and in scope than that allowed by any library technical-processes department. It is fairly obvious that we must look to the academic to continue our own specialty. We wish to find that individual who is comfortable in the world of ideas, who enjoys the academic life, and who holds such a life as an ideal. We are looking for converts or disciples who will be satisfied in an austerity that fortunately is somewhat more worldly than monastic.

At present it is a life that has the odor of sanctity about it, or, at least in these times of lush extravagance, there is a chance of one's patches showing. Our librarian lives are becoming less threadbare, but, in comparison with the trades —let alone the professions—we do exude an air of penury that comes neither from musty books nor from a consecrated de-

[11] L. Powell, "Education for Academic Librarianship," in *Education for Librarianship: Papers Presented at the Library Conference, University of Chicago, August 16–21, 1948*, ed. Bernard Berelson (Chicago: American Library Association, 1949), p. 137.

votion to our calling. And this is relevant to the search for recruits, for we can offer neither fine pecuniary rewards nor a great and compensating respect for the profession. In the face of materialistic standards that nearly envelop us, we can offer only the academic life. To those who have a conviction that education is very important, to those who like to teach and to learn, to those who like to associate with books and students and faculty, we can give haven. The individual who enjoys the leisure to explore ideas can obtain it in the college. Not for a minute do I suggest that the college librarian or professor works less than a forty-hour week; on the contrary, I mean to imply that here one's working hours are endless and indistinguishable from one's leisure. But the pace is not so rapid as in business, and there is not the pressure of a report of progress on one's every move. Our atmosphere is a continuation of those happy and presumably carefree days of a college career where it is not wicked to inform one's self about the nature of the Pre-Raphaelites, for example, even if one happens to be a chemistry major. Such excursions are called "building a cultural background," and this kind of knowledge can be very useful in a librarian while it enriches his associations with students.

These desirable people do exist, for we are continually drawing new and good librarians into the fold. They come, of course, primarily from the colleges themselves. They are nurtured and forwarded to the library schools from the colleges by the good and understanding professor and the enlightened and enthusiastic librarian. Librarians teaching courses have the best and widest influence. The subject matter need not be library theory, for the courses may be in English, such as those Mr. McKeon holds, or in bibliography, like those Mr. Julian Fowler schedules. All the staff of the library have an opportunity to impress and inspire by personal word and deed those students who work in the library as assistants. In this regard it seems as if more could be done with student assistants to capture and hold their youthful and impetuous enthusiasms. Have we given the promising student a proper chance to exercise his ingenuity by allowing him varied experience, opportunity for initiative, such as preparing exhibits or selecting books for purchase, or exercise of some responsibility perchance in regard to publicity? Or have we kept him attaching bookplates and pockets until the paste runs out of his ears and he runs out of the library for good? We can and must capitalize on this great and continuing source of librarian material.

Another potential source of librarians within the college is the faculty itself. Have we tapped those instructors who are not entirely at ease in thier profession of teaching? The library can offer a great deal to some professors who have widely ranging interests in books. William Dix, the new Princeton librarian, is a fine example of a good professor who became completely intrigued with the library, to the definite enhancement of our profession. Branscomb, who has seen the problem from all sides, cites two types of faculty members to whom the library might appeal: (1) the man who does not enjoy lecturing but who is intrigued by the bibliography of his subject and (2) the man who is interested in administration and looks to the general problems and objectives of his campus.

The library has concern with nearly every aspect of the college, for its literature cuts across all departmental barriers. Even the athletic department can be indebted to the library for the choice of books on sports, while the librarian could appropriately serve on the faculty athletic committee, a duty I once enjoyed. The administration and business offices call upon the library for information and advice. Archives, theater, fraternity, and alumni should involve the library. In fact, the librarian ought to have a hand in almost everything that transpires. Surely this wide base of operations offers a place for people of varied talent on campus who might wish to transfer to the library.

There is yet another source of possible librarians worth investigating. Occasionally the world of business casts out a first-rate person. Possibly this is more accurately stated if we say that some unusual individuals are unhappy enough to get out or, at least, to contemplate and escape from the system. Usually such people, and they are few, have rather wide cultural interests and are not satisfied in a business milieu. Fortunately, they are usually well qualified in educational background and travel when they come to the librarian for counsel. For them the librarian can only pose the financial dilemma, which may end the matter unless they have supplementary means. However, these questing souls should not be repulsed merely because they have not been subjected to the boredom of the endless routines that the average neophyte has endured. Some have very useful special experience as book collectors or booksellers, and they all have an embarrassingly exalted attitude toward our trade.

For these library enthusiasts, whether they come from teaching or business or leisure, we have made very few allowances. I am referring now to the educated and experienced adult who desires, for good and sufficient reason, to become a librarian. Some few have money and fortitude enough to take a one-year library degree, and there are many happy instances, increasingly so in these days, of valuable additions to our profession by this means. They enrich our trade by their varied experiences and varying perspectives in a way that can broaden and deepen our concept of librarianship.

This may be an appropriate time to relax our standards to let in a few carefully chosen individuals who lack their union cards. I hasten to state that I am referring only to the specialized field of college-library personnel. Most of us would agree with Branscomb that a little teaching is not a bad thing for a college librarian and that the library is rewarded by any specialization a librarian may care to develop. In our need for scholarly personnel, may we court the intrigued and educated individual with a short-term course in library school? Personalities we would like to attract to college-library work are sometimes put off by what they visualize as a stultifying year devoted to techniques. They may be justified in believing that a Master's degree in a subject field is comparable to a Master's in library service when they cite that the librarian's beginning salary is equivalent to that of a college instructor's. We might allow the individual we truly desire to take a formalized short course of a summer or a quarter, to acquire rapidly the theory in cataloging, reference, and bibliography necessary for trained library personnel. In effect, colleges sometimes do this— either by design or through desperation —when they give a professional position to an instructor or a faculty wife, with the understanding that library theory can be acquired during vacations, just as teachers procure temporary certificates to teach before completing all

requisites. Possibly this is a poor comparison, for I do not wish to suggest that our colleges are in any way bound by formal requirements similar to those which teachers' colleges certify for their personnel. It is at once a strength and a glory that our institutions of higher education are not bound by the *education* requirements that take up such a large proportion of the program for secondary-school teachers. College teachers are chosen not on the basis of the number of hours they have satisfied in education but on their competency in a chosen field. The librarian, administering for the college, is not bound by the state laws of standardization, and his appointment of an expert need not conform to the extent of holding a library degree.

There is no doubt of the body of knowledge that librarians must acquire to be able to do their jobs effectively. Experimentation is wasteful when organized experience is readily available in classes of library administration and organization and in cataloging and classifying methods. Courses in reference tools and in general and subject bibliography are the best way to build the wide technical proficiency necessary in library work. Surveys of the history of books and libraries, of the development of printing, of the myriad processes of reproduction, and of the craft of bookbinding and repair are all useful to librarians. For all these things one goes to library school and is rewarded by a superficial knowledge that is impressive to the uninitiated. Thereafter, it is the individual's responsibility to continue his studies in some branch to gain the depth that gives lasting satisfaction.

If one must choose between technical proficiency (which is all some of our library-school products have) and scholarly qualities of mind, Branscomb would choose the scholar, on the principle that it is easier to add the technical training to scholarship than to superimpose scholarship on specialized training. He believes: "Given the scholarly outlook and training and the proper personal qualifications—among which a decent humility stands very high—the technical training can be acquired either by attendance at library school, or by assiduous study of the literature, along with practical experience."[12] Three distinguished librarians extended this by going on record before the Carnegie Corporation in 1931 as believing that "specialized scholarship with or without library school training is always likely to form a basis for appointment to higher positions in the library profession."[13] Apparently, subsequent appointments have tended to justify their opinion. These are strong words and certainly a provocative challenge to the profession.

There are serious hazards in the kind of recruitment just described which might be characterized as proselytizing. One must guard against the maladjusted, the floater, the failure, and the flashy. Library work is too important these days to offer a refuge for the incompetent or a sinecure for the lazy. There is danger, too, in the multitude of trivia that can be unearthed in a library, for we do not want the kind of people who are likely to fritter their time away on minutiae. This weakness ought to be discernible, but it may develop at a later date as a method of avoiding undesirable work. I remember a head librarian who spent a goodly proportion of her time carefully winding skeins of every piece of string that came into the college library.

Another mania which we discern in our staffs is the tendency to lock up the books and to be stingy with the loan periods of those that do circulate. Librarian Sibley may have been in step with the nineteenth-century Harvard faculty when he rushed after the last book not back on the library shelves; but now we all wish to get the books out to anyone who shows the slightest interest in them. We will be well advised to get the martinet out of the library also, for we must court the casual reader, in addition to giving the freedom of the house to the serious scholar.

There is danger for today's librarian because the technical routines may take priority, thus submerging scholarship. There is, of course, room for the pure administrator in certain positions within the larger libraries. However, there must be some balanced bookmen to check on the technical enthusiasms, so that the library is not entirely disrupted by slavery to an IBM machine. Equally hazardous is the likelihood that the book-minded may take too complete refuge behind the books. We all know of the librarian who disappears into the stacks, to reappear many hours later empty-handed and maybe empty-minded. John Quincy Adams, in planning the facilities of the Smithsonian Institution, put this matter with some force: "and above all no jobbing—no sinecures—no monkish stalls for lazy idlers."[14]

In fact, we want the best personnel possible, and we are limited by the material available. This was expressed early in library-school history by Melvil Dewey, who I am sure has been quoted here before. He said:

[12] Branscomb, *op. cit.*, pp. 89–90.

[13] Carnegie Corporation of New York, *Report of Informal Conferences on Library Interests, December 8, 1930* (New York: Carnegie Corporation, 1931), pp. 46–47.

[14] Quoted from his *Diary*, June 24, 1838, in *Smithsonian Misc. Coll.*, XVII, 767.

The library school is weak in many of its graduates, but, as I say to every class, we can only find out what is in the people who come to us. If a man is born of poor fibre, of poor fibre he will remain; you can polish an agate, you can polish mahogany, but you can't polish a pumpkin—and if a third-rate man comes to a library school, and the Lord made him third-rate, he will be a third-rate librarian to the end of the chapter.[15]

There is even the less likely probability that the candidate will be too good. Those librarians who teach may find themselves loaded with a complete schedule of class hours while they unobtrusively slip off the library payroll. This is quite understandable, for the teaching faculty forms the elite in the college—professors are in close fraternity, while the librarians may be out on a peninsula, in some institutions, at least, in the regard of the students. Administration, too, calls some of our best people, and we observe with pride that deans and college presidents may once have been college librarians. A past president of A.L.A., Errett McDiarmid, is now dean of sciences, literature, and the arts at Minnesota; Robert McEwen, once librarian-professor at Carleton, is now president of Hamilton; while Harvie Branscomb went from the post of director of libraries at Duke to the chancellorship of Vanderbilt.

There are steps we can take toward the perfect state when just the ideal person fills the post of college librarian. This large wish reminds me of the Kentuckian and his nearly perfect coon-dog. The farmer had merely to prop a board for stretching a skin of a particular size against the barn and his dog would sniff the board and go off and tree a coon of just the proper dimensions. This procedure worked without a hitch for all the different-size skin-stretchers the farm-

[15] *Library Journal*, XXV (August, 1900), 112.

er owned, until the day his wife left her ironing board against the barn. The dog took a sniff, went off, and never returned. We must not be discouraged by the gap between the progress we would wish to make and our present dimensions. It takes gradual and also slow progress to raise the level within the profession to the station where we truly merit the respect we desire from all quarters.

In recruiting we can be more selective and at the same time both charitable and ingenious in raiding other callings. We have a dignified profession that offers great variety and prestige to its members—we can be very proud to invite others we admire to join us. We can be more considerate of student assistants and give some special experience to the promising ones. In our staffs we can give more responsibility and encouragement to those members who show initiative as prospects for library school or for positions of greater trust and variety. On the other hand, we must also protect our staffs from an absorption with needless detail or wholly technical concerns, for today in the library the human aspect can and should take precedence over the mechanical. For the lazy professional who has eased back to let others do it, we can urge special projects that demand finite results—such as preparing bibliographies or exhibits or the writing of articles, for the holding up of one's work to the criticism of colleagues either at home or abroad is a humbling and yet exhilarating process. Exchange of personnel here and abroad can certainly prevent rigidity and should foster new attitudes of work and of living.

To take his intended place on the campus, the librarian must be intimately aware of the educational objectives not only of the college but also of each department and, if possible, of every professor. The library can stand as vital to the college only as the librarians involve the library in every aspect of the college both within and without the curriculum. Not only can exhibits be tied in with courses, but library-prepared bibliographies can help the library take its role of importance in the college. While most professors want the library to take a more active part in the college life, the librarians have been hanging back. At least, they have been so concerned with building the book collection—a universal failing—that for the most part they have nearly neglected to use what they do have. Now that we are moving into a period of selectivity, perhaps more consideration will be given to the teaching function of the library and, incidentally, of the library staff.

Our library schools might consider putting more guts in their courses by offering more scholarly fare. Classes in paleography, graphic arts, archival methods, and courses on books themselves would satisfy neglected areas in the university and would provoke definite interest from other departments. The library-school professor must recognize the scholarly minded and encourage them in college and university work. This has been the case in the past, but we must guard against a drift toward public library work, primarily for salary considerations.

There is still much to be done in regard to salaries. Remarkable progress has been made in the last decades, but there is room for improvement. Salaries ought to be more nearly commensurate with the amount of time spent in acquiring the basic educational requirements. As a profession, the library profession ought to be measured and paid by standards that apply to other professions.

Librarians enjoy a fine regard in the United States. Certain areas of our concern touch the entire nation's consciousness, such as the freedom to read statements indorsed last June at Los Angeles. We have close ties with educators and publishers. Our indexes are used and appreciated by novice and scholar alike. Our most natural alliance is with books, for we are keepers of books. Archibald MacLeish gives us our true mission as he differentiates between two kinds of books:

The physical book is never more than an ingenious and often beautiful cipher by which the intellectual book is communicated from one mind to another. . . . The intellectual book is a construction of the spirit, and the constructions of the spirit exist in one time only—in that continuing and endless present which is now. If it is the intellectual book rather than the physical book of which the librarian is the keeper, then the profession of the librarian is not and cannot be the neutral, passive, negative profession of the guardian and fiduciary, but must become instead the affirmative and advocating profession of the attorney for a cause. For the intellectual book is the word. And the keepers of the word, whether they so choose or not, must be its partisans and advocates.[16]

[16] Archibald MacLeish, *A Time To Speak* . . . , (Boston: Houghton Mifflin Co., 1941), pp. 27–29.

THE PLACE OF NEWER MEDIA IN THE UNDER-
GRADUATE PROGRAM

C. WALTER STONE

AUDIO-VISUAL service has become an established part of most American college and university programs. It is maintained by various agencies, some of which operate with full independence of other administrative units. In some institutions, audio-visual services are centered in libraries; in others, they are concentrated in special departments tied administratively, and often functionally in the sense of a teaching laboratory, to schools of education or journalism, divisions of university extension, or similar campus units. Except in a few smaller colleges having new or remodeled library buildings, audio-visual centers differ little, regardless of the sponsor. A change of pattern is needed, and perhaps the best time to accomplish such a change in libraries comes when a new building is in prospect.

This paper challenges traditional plans for audio-visual service to the undergraduate program and presents a point of view which looks in other directions. It is hoped that comparable thinking will precede the laying of specific plans for college-library service with audio-visual materials and equipment on many a campus where the librarian is now moving toward his drawing board. The speaker acknowledges gratefully the help of librarians and directors of audio-visual service agencies in several parts of the United States who have been kind enough to write him about the place of newer media in the undergraduate programs they know best.

INTRODUCTION

Films, filmstrips, slides, sound recordings, and an array of other nonprint materials, including maps, pictures, charts, graphics, models, exhibits, and mockups, constitute some of the newer media of communication. Normally they are classed together and referred to by educators as "audio-visual materials." For administrative comfort or perhaps resulting from administrative laziness and disregarding logic entirely, the numerous mechanical and electronic devices which implement diagrammatic, pictorial, and oral communication intended primarily for groups are also added to this aggregation—i.e., radio, television, and a wide variety of optical systems for magnification and projection, as well as more prosaic tools—felt boards, chalk boards, tachistoscopes, and microcard readers. In short, the newer media are customarily defined so as to incorporate all communication materials and the equipment for their use, apart from books or other media which utilize the written or printed page. This situation is unfortunate and has been caused in part by excessive pride and ignorance among both librarians and nonlibrary audio-visual specialists and too much separate on-campus promotion of newer media as the result of imagined competition with the old.

Those who embrace newer media most enthusiastically are prone to minimize the contributions of print. Others, primarily book-oriented, claim the newer

84

media are uncomfortable to use, expensive in time and money to acquire, difficult to administer, and require too much specialized knowledge and skill to be worth the trouble of learning to produce and use for educational purposes. Neither position is logically tenable, but both receive the kind of rationalized justification which is normally put forward during a period of adjustment to new social or technical ways. A frequent result has been that two libraries have developed on the campus of the large college or university. One assumes full responsibility for print, and the other tries to obtain a proprietary interest in everything else. Borderline cases, such as equipment for photo reproduction and microphotography, are settled on the bases of space available, personalities, and budget. If radio, television, publication, and graphic services are not already attached to established academic departments as laboratories or teaching units, they, too, may be regarded as proper candidates for administration by the nonbook library. On a smaller campus, which usually cannot afford the luxury of two centers for storage and distribution of communications materials, there may be greater interest in a merger. The pattern may be one either of a book library and decentralized nonbook services or of gradual assimilation of all media into the book library, physically and perhaps administratively, but almost certainly perpetuating the illogic of a separate department for nonprint materials and equipment. Arguments given to justify this practice derive from precedents represented in other library division by form, from lack of an interested staff trained to work with newer media, or from some assumed needs for centralized storage and maintenance of audio-visual

materials and equipment. Local conditions will change the pattern slightly, but, whether in or out of the book library, distinctions between print and nonprint materials are clung to desperately. When such distinctions have broken down, a media specialist may be employed to work, for example, in the departmental music library with its collection of classical recordings. Even here, too often, one is likely to find nonmusical recordings of everything from radio programs and commencement addresses to sound effects shelved next to Brahms, Beethoven, and Schubert.

It is a primary thesis of this paper that undue observance of form distinctions seriously handicaps library service to higher education; that a unified subject or problem cross-media approach to knowledge is most efficient for the undergraduate student as well as for his teacher; and that this approach will ultimately prove the most satisfactory to administer in terms of the media themselves. This proposition is not widely tested in experience, although many major colleges and universities, including Stanford, Harvard, Purdue, and Illinois, apply its principles at least in part. It is also an assumption of the speaker that (with a few exceptions taken to fit local situations) original production of new teaching materials—films, slides, books, television programs, and the like—should not be considered a primary responsibility of the library. Finally, by way of completing this introduction, it is thought unnecessary at this conference to cite lengthy researches which would give supporting evidence in behalf of psychological and other advantages accruing to learning from the effective use of audio-visual materials.

EXTENT OF SERVICE

The role of newer media in the under-graduate program has expanded greatly during recent years. This is so for a number of reasons: individual faculty initiative, slow methodological seepages from departments of teacher education or vocational schools (via cross-fertilizing intra-institutional subcellar or "coffee-hour" channels); a recent influx of younger instructors who do not easily remember days before the motion picture and radio; evident broadening of interests among commercial producers and improvement in their materials; academic competition for educational contracts from the government; the press of post–World War II acceleration and general enlargement of facilities for higher education; and some remarkably successful experiments in mass education begun during the war and continued internationally in subsequent efforts in behalf of world improvement and rehabilitation. Also important have been military and commercial demands and precedents for increasing the speed and breadth of technical training, by presenting the talents of the best available teachers via new media, and a major overhauling, immediate expansion, and rapid growth since 1946 of the audio-visual equipment industry.

These are a few of the things which since 1945 have brought about major changes in the methods and the materials of instruction used on the college campus in more traditional, as well as newer, divisions of instruction. Such changes do not appear systematically, resulting more often, it would seem, from happenstance than planning and from presidential desires to keep up with the academic Joneses or maintain accreditation and from outside pressure. But the rate of their appearance has increased

steadily. Figures gathered in a survey of audio-visual services in colleges and universities in the United States, undertaken in March, 1952, by the Association of Colleges and Research Libraries, show that more than four-fifths of about 575 institutions which replied to a questionnaire maintain some established unit on the campus to provide audio-visual service. A third of the reporting institutions maintain centralized agencies for distribution of newer media, and half of these are housed in libraries. As a matter of interest, while these figures are being reported, more than half the college and university librarians who replied, (58 per cent) indorsed a statement that the library should administer and service *all materials of communication, including audio-visual materials.* Another interesting set of statistics taken from this same report revealed that 99 per cent of the centralized separate audio-visual agencies and 87 per cent of libraries maintaining audio-visual service provide films. Ninety-three per cent of the separate agencies and 90 per cent of the library centers give service with filmstrips. And, quoting directly, "eighty-nine per cent of the library centers include recordings in their service patterns, while 70 per cent of the separate A-V agencies give service with recordings. A majority of each type of center handles slides, but whereas approximately two-thirds of the library centers render service with maps and pictures, a little over one-fourth of the separate agencies service these materials."[1] The newer media ranked in order of attention given them by these college audio-visual service

[1] A.C.R.L. Committee on Audio-visual Work, "Audio-visual Services in Colleges and Universities in the United States" (unpublished) (Tucson: The Committee, 1953), p. 11.

units are (1) the motion picture, (2) the filmstrip, (3) sound recordings, (4) slides, (5) flat pictures, and (6) maps, with provision of other materials not recorded.

The figures given above tell only the number of institutions offering such service. Quantitative data on frequency of use of various types of materials for curricular purposes and sizes and costs of maintaining collections would be equally significant, if not more so. Such figures are not readily at hand, and, at best, they would have only temporary value. However, a handbook is now being written for publication next year by the College and University Section of the Division of Audio-visual Instruction of the National Education Association, which will try to cover these points and thoroughly describe operations of nonbook audio-visual libraries. Its figures obviously will not establish the preeminence of one material over another or impute to one teaching department more audio-visual sense or sensitivity than to another, since requirements differ. But they will show reliably, I hope, certain normal fiscal arrangements, and the proportionate demand for nonprint materials and service of the departments serving the typical undergraduate program. Parenthetically, referring back to arguments for and against separate agency versus library administration of audio-visual services, I might add at this point that separate agencies have tended to develop audio-visual services mainly in terms of films, filmstrips, tape recordings, and recording and projection equipment, whereas libraries generally offer more diversified service with materials but have, to an appreciable extent, ignored campus needs for motion pictures, filmstrips, and audio-visual equipment.

METHODS OF USE

For what purposes are the newer media used in the undergraduate program? Without quoting from texts on teaching methods or presenting the evidence of several hundred significant studies of learning from audio-visual materials, it may suffice to state that all media of communication are used in teaching, to help to enrich the learning process. The educational advantages of using what we are pleased here to call the "newer media" stem from their physical nature, that is, their rather obvious capacity conveniently to provide experiences more closely approximating those of direct face-to-face contact. In some cases they go beyond, to provide insights into abstract concepts not readily grasped by other means. An example of this point is the present widespread use of animated motion pictures to present concepts of atomic fission or operation of new mechanical and electronic devices. Slow-motion and time-lapse photography have opened the door to wholly new popular understanding of our natural world and made clear to millions for the first time the true nature of plant and animal growth. The ability of the motion picture and sound recording to re-create history and conveniently edit time and space are well known. The question posed most frequently is: Under what circumstances are they the best means for so doing? Here comparisons are usually made with economies of print.

Without discussing scientifically factors of greater interest stimulation, factual retention, influence on values or appreciation which may be induced by the new media, it is recognized that an individual who has never heard an opera or seen a great painting or, to illustrate from another field, observed children at play will develop little understanding or appreciation of these simply from reading about them. He needs a more direct tie with experience before he can handle abstract generalizations or formulate reliably his own judgments concerning their worth. Thus in fields where direct and common experience may be lacking in a class or when it is unusual, impossible, or inconvenient to achieve, the newer media are found very useful in providing edited versions of the experiences required. On the other hand, elaborate audio-visual documentation of an experience commonly known is a gross waste of time. It is much better to re-create or recall such experience in the most economical way, that is, usually with verbal symbols.

In addition to providing convenient and necessary substitutes for direct experience (substitutes which at times can be more significant, safer, or richer in the provision of aesthetic satisfactions than direct experience itself), the newer media have produced artistic and cultural forms which should be studied for appreciation on their own terms. If we are to help undergraduates develop good taste in media selection and have full knowledge of the presentational capacities of the various media of communication and their potentialities for artistic achievement, as well as social influence, it is essential to teach discrimination. This can be accomplished only by exposure to a fairly broad range of the products of the media under competent guidance. To cite just one example, on the college level an increasing number of courses, as well as informal meetings and forums, are being given over to discussion of the history, nature, technique, and social contribution of the motion picture. The library's contribution through noon-hour concerts, public forums, and general film showings open to the college community at large has been significant.

Any complete inventory of ways in which newer media are used in the classroom, laboratory, or seminar to implement the study of undergraduates would be monotonous to repeat and irritating to hear. It is in order, however, to report a few current examples to illustrate uses of the media in various subject fields. Detailed summaries of such uses will be found in the Stephens College reports of its annual conference on effective utilization of audio-visual materials in college teaching. Others may be located by consulting the brief general list of references appended to this paper.

In teaching composition, rhetoric, English literature, and communication arts, much use is currently being made of opaque projection equipment to facilitate class discussion and criticism of individual or sample themes. At Wayne University in Detroit, a composition clinic draws heavily on prerecorded tapes to help students practice structuring sentences at their leisure without tying up the precious time of instructors. Educational films—and reduced or, occasionally, the full-length version of a theatrical motion picture—are exhibited to help develop appreciation of the cinema or to provide a background for discussion of a literary period. Undergraduates listen to recordings of plays, as well as read and talk about them— materials ranging from the works of Shakespeare to those of T. S. Eliot and Arthur Miller.

A collection of recordings of famous poets reading their own verses is one of the major contributions to the field of literature and speech made at Harvard by Professor Frederick Packard. Harvard boasts the college library's best-known collection of this type, the remarkable Harvard Vocarium, housed originally in the Lamont Library, in a suite of rooms especially designed for comfortable private enjoyment and study of written as well as auditory texts of a broad range of prose, drama, poetry, and folk material.

Contemporary methods for improvement of reading and oral skills depend heavily on applications of the newer media. Showing the Harvard reading films in conjunction with the use of other devices, such as tachistoscopes utilizing both commercially prepared and homemade slides, and use of the pacer is standard practice. Filmstrips are being produced at Minnesota for use in a new "control reader projector." Speech departments denied access to an extensive library of recordings and recording facilities of their own are almost unknown these days. Growing use of opaque projectors is being made in speech and theater arts departments for study of photographs and drawings of stage and costume design. Locally produced films and kinescopes are made available for group study and appreciation or self-criticism of theatrical performances.

The modern foreign-language department also relies upon newer media to assist both classroom instruction and individual study. Supplementing slides, flat pictures, opaque projection of special materials, objects, exhibits, transcriptions of foreign radio programs, and the like, much use is made of motion pictures, tape recordings, and student recording facilities. A new range of listening booths was recently constructed at Ohio State University to improve the efficiency of language instruction and individual study. Wayne University claims larger enrolments and better instruction

in French as the result of the carefully planned use of recording devices and a cultural backgrounding process abetted by slides, films, and filmstrips. A unique application of the motion picture in teaching a foreign language has been the production (again at Wayne) of films with foreign-language sound tracks having various narration speeds and levels of vocabulary difficulty. The English version of one such film, *Le Mont Saint Michel*, produced from footage taken by a Wayne instructor, is currently being distributed nationally for its pictorial content alone (which is a rather happy means for the university to finance an otherwise expensive project). Sound-stripping—that is, local recording on a narrow strip of magnetic tape attached to a motion picture to replace or supplement the original sound track, if any, of a film—is used to accomplish the same goal at Southern Illinois University in Carbondale. Wayne's library of tapes, individual cubicles, and foreign-language classroom, in which each student has a microphone plugged into a master-wire recorder, and its use of double-headed tape recorders to enable students to interpolate answers to prerecorded questions, appear to have accelerated, as well as improved measurably, the quality of both instruction and learning, and they have been copied widely. Incidentally, the librarian's problem of deciding what materials and equipment to handle in this area seems no more difficult than that of making similar decisions with regard to more traditional laboratories—physics, chemistry, botany, biology, geology, etc.

One of the most interesting foreign-language laboratories is that established in 1951 at Purdue. It may be worth while to describe the Purdue program in some detail as a means of summarizing the use of the newer media to expedite teaching programs in this field. Costing a scant fifteen thousand dollars to construct and equip fully, the Purdue laboratory contains twenty-eight individual semi-soundproof booths. Each booth is equipped with its own tape recorder, earphones, and microphone, and all booths are tied to master-control units at the front of the room. One opaque projector and a speed reader present the visual materials needed for a given lesson. The basic procedure in the laboratory has been described in this way: "A page or story in the textbook is first put on film. Then the instructor, in advance, projects the film at the desired speed, and reading aloud from the screen, he records it on tape. When the class meets, the students read the text on the screen while they hear the same text coming through their earphones."[2] This procedure is varied according to need. One group may wish to see repeated showings of the same text at greater speeds accompanied by synchronous oral texts. Another class may alternate visual with auditory presentation. There can be timed pauses in presentation, while students write out or record on tape what they have just seen or heard. Visual presentation in the foreign language with English tapes or vice versa is another variant frequently used.

A final hint which may demonstrate the alpha and omega of using recordings in the field of language arts was demonstrated last fall in New Haven, Connecticut. Commencing with an examination given to 300 Freshmen, Yale University used tape-recorded foreign-language materials to test the conversational as well as the reading and writing abilities of

students. The entire procedure, including instructions to students, was carried out in French, and, according to a recent announcement, copies of this examination will be used in fourteen other colleges during 1954.

A recent survey of "Big Ten" colleges and universities indicates that in teaching world history, political science, and the social sciences generally, an adequate library of pertinent films, filmstrips, slides, and recordings has become essential, and major increases in demand for audio-visual service are being recorded. At the University of Illinois a departmental collection of films presenting case studies and special demonstrations are shown regularly to undergraduate classes in psychology. In sociology and anthropology much has been done by many universities with film material, especially in using some of the early documentary films to introduce studies of cultural patterns and family life. Philosophy, religion, the humanities, and even history (history is probably the one department having the greatest antipathy to unwritten records unless they be artifacts) afford numerous examples of imaginative and valuable reference to newer media. The production and group use of special sound filmstrips, in company with charts, graphs, and written outlines, have been pioneered at the schools of Labor and Industrial Relations at Rutgers and Cornell. In political science classes, interviews with prominent persons, prerecorded on tape, furnish the basis for class discussion of urgent contemporary problems.

Recording the talks of visiting lecturers is common university practice. Less familiar may be Kent State's use of recorded lectures for critical self-evaluation of an instructor's performance (not a bad idea!). Pennsylvania State College

[2] Elton Hocking, "The Power of Babel," *Educational Screen*, XXX (December, 1951), 40.

has developed a library of films and tape recordings which are used to demonstrate the symptoms of mental illness. Taped collections of short-wave radio broadcasts are being introduced to students of advertising, propaganda, and radio journalism. Perhaps these examples, cited almost at random, offer sufficient evidence of use in the fields named.

The physical and biological sciences, as well as vocational and professional fields, have long made use of commercial as well as homemade films, slides and other transparencies, exhibits, specimens, microprojectors, etc., to assist comprehension of basic ideas. Applications in these fields are as diversified as there are instructors with ingenuity and willingness to give time to the adaptation of existing materials or the preparation of new ones. To illustrate, one audio-visual service furnishes its astronomy department with a sizable library of homemade slides to show star clusters. Holes punched in $3\frac{1}{2} \times 4$-inch sheets of laundry cardboard, when projected by a standard slide projector, produce the illusion. Finding a lack of suitable commercially prepared material to present some scientific and highly technical material, Purdue University is making quite a business of producing short, tailor-made films which present the information needed and nothing else. The University of Illinois recently wanted an efficient means of teaching students in chemistry to use the analytical balance. The solution, which would show completely in full magnification and "close-up" detail the proper procedures, was a film, produced a few months ago.

Athletic coaches, as well as instructors in business colleges, have found loop films a convenient aid for study of time-and-motion operations. Students of mathematics and their friends in engineering make intensive use of films, slides, filmstrips, cut-away sections, models, and three-dimensional drawings. "Layup" or "strip-tease" presentations on the felt board are equally familiar and useful in outlining organizational structure, explaining color keying, or defining geometric figures. Science survey courses use an overhead or opaque projector to show simple chemical reactions of living specimens. The resulting large image on a suitable screen is sharp, clear, and reproduced in full color. The place of newer media in the undergraduate program is well established.

TELEVISION

The invitation which led to this paper asked, among other questions, "What is likely to be the true role (as distinguished from an enthusiast's current definition) of films, pictures, slides, sound recordings, television, etc., in the college instructional program?" I still do not know how to answer this question, because most enthusiasts tend to limit their interest to only one or two areas and to promote the use of one medium—say, filmstrips. You may have heard such a person say, "The best way to teach anything is with filmstrips." And if you have ever run across an enthusiast for educational exhibits or one who is a zealot for field trips, you know how ardent and annoying such people can be. In my opinion—perhaps a surprising one to this group—the trouble with most such enthusiasts is that they fall far short of the truth. I would agree that the place of newer media in the undergraduate program is at present modest, although I do not agree with one audio-visual specialist and authority on reading methods who has stated that college applications of the newer media are less frequent and imaginative than any others. I believe the limits are still unknown, and I think, frankly, that at this time the future depends more upon factors of physical housing of materials and equipment, budgets, production facilities, bibliographic and distribution systems, faculty education, and student readiness than upon any intrinsic characteristics of the media. A few words about television may clarify this point, and then we shall consider some of the problems just raised from the viewpoint of a college library.

Omitting consideration of new processes for instantaneous reproduction in facsimile, television and TV tape are probably the newest of the new media which have already invaded the campus or will shortly do so. The story of commercial television's development and Athena-like industrial birth in 1948; its subsequent spread across the nation in six years, to command, in 1954, an audience of more than five million Americans for major productions; and its eyewitness accounts of United Nations sessions, political conventions and inaugurations, Senate committee hearings, full-length operas as well as sporting events, comedy and drama, millions of feet of once (and, I should add, very wisely) discarded theatrical films, the foam of beer advertisements and many of the more disgusting aspects of mass-media exploitation, are familiar and have been well told elsewhere. Education's attempt to capture and hold at least a portion of the broadcast spectrum for regular and continuing programming by educators trained for effective use of the medium, thanks to the beneficence of the Ford Foundation and a nationally organized citizen effort, now seems destined to achieve some success, despite

low educational budgets, commercial efforts at sabotage, a surplus of raw, untrained recruits, and dire predictions that educational TV will eventually go the way of education by radio through academic default. Experiments conducted by universities and colleges in co-operation with commercial stations in New York, Philadelphia, Baltimore, Cleveland, Detroit, Chicago, and elsewhere across the country have served as proving grounds, and advance knowledge of the fruits of their experience will save many new ventures from failure. Public support of college credit courses conducted by TV is "small potatoes" when measured by commercial standards for audiences. But it is phenomenal for higher education. Experiments with such courses at Western Reserve and the University of Michigan have led these institutions to devote sizable budgets to TV, and one midwestern college sees such promise in televised assistance for its program of agricultural extension that approximately half the extension funds allocated for this year are being used to launch a full-scale program. Typical of the "tele-course" movement were some programs conducted (after four years of preliminary experimentation) over station WEWS in Cleveland. Two courses, on comparative literature and general psychology, were broadcast Tuesday and Thursday mornings from nine to nine-thirty. End-of-course examinations given to those enrolled in campus classes in the same subjects did not show as much gain as did those graded for students taking the course at home via TV. Figures compiled more recently on six "tele-courses" offered for three hours' credit each show that, during a thirteen-week period, more than 100,000 people watched a part of the series. Mail responses for a single program might exceed 1,500 units; and in one course in which there were 108 credit enrolments 700 syllabi were sold. The total cost to Western Reserve of putting on these courses, including salaries, clerical expenses, and publication, was approximately $11,000. Revenues from enrolments and sale of publications totaled nearly $13,000. The age range of students enrolled in the "tele-courses" was from nineteen to sixty-eight, with a median age of thirty-seven.

Among educational television stations, WOI-TV, in Iowa, has pioneered in the field of higher and general adult education for more than twenty years. KUHT at the University of Houston in Texas, KUSC at the University of Southern California in Los Angeles, and WKAR-TV at Michigan State in East Lansing were the first three noncommercial television stations to get under way. More will follow shortly. Drains on staff time (in order to program 42 hours weekly in East Lansing, for example) and educational budgets will be enormous, even for such co-operative TV ventures as channel 11 in Chicago and channel 56 in Detroit. To put these stations on the air will eventually cost nearly a million and a quarter dollars each, and annual operating budgets are very conservatively estimated at from $100,000 to $250,000. It is believed by those promoting such stations—for example, the sponsors of channel 56 in Detroit—that the combined efforts of the several universities, libraries, museums, and other educational agencies who will share production responsibilities will manage a spread of worth-while cultural, informative, and educational materials to tens of thousands who are otherwise normally denied access to such material and may, in weeks and months, accomplish goals of public enlighten-

ment which formerly were not feasible with any expenditures of time and money before TV. If this sounds improperly enthusiastic, I apologize. I mean only to be factual. Nor should we forget or minimize dangers and the real threats of misuse and abuse and/or neglect by educators of television as well as of the other newer media of communication. We may note in passing that television has an insatiable appetite for all audio-visual materials.

Two recent college-sponsored uses of TV may hold special interest for this group. During the summer of 1953, station KTYL-TV in Tempe, Arizona, broadcast an experimental series of programs initiated by the reading clinic at Arizona State College. Called "Let's Read Better," this program was designed to test the possibility of using various clinical devices, such as the tachistoscope and the various mechanical reading accelerators, through the medium. This series was planned by Rexford Bolling, director of the reading clinic, and Richard H. Bell, Radio-TV director of the college. Among closed-circuit experiments (that is, local television via wires and cables), those in progress at Chicago Teachers College are worthy of special note. Here small TV camera units (now used commonly for observation of industrial processes not safe for human beings or directly accessible to them) are wired to as many as ten ordinary 17-, 21-, and 24-inch TV receivers and used to show enlarged views of models, dissections, techniques of an artist, or other operations immediately under class discussion. Why not use film? Costs of production and processing, the desire of lecturers to vary materials and their demonstration techniques, and the inconvenience of projection are valid replies.

To give further consideration to live broadcasting of television programs, there are several straws in the wind which have implications for "universities on the air." First, a small but significant event—the United States Department of Agriculture recently established a Film Clip Library to service land-grant colleges and others using agricultural motion-picture footage for TV. Funds from the Ford and Kellogg foundations and from universities are being spread widely across the country for the establishment of new educational film centers and production of films for television uniquely appropriate for production by the institutions concerned by reason of geography, personnel, or other special resources. Many of these films and film series, some of which will be made by kinescopic techniques— that is, filming of live TV programs—will be sent to the Educational Radio and Television Center established by the Ford Foundation's Fund for Adult Education in Ann Arbor, Michigan. There prints will be duplicated as necessary and sent out for use on educational TV stations. The end-result will simulate network operations at a low cost. Good material produced in Atlanta will be available for broadcasting in Urbana and Seattle when and as needed, and the consequent development of local kinescope libraries will simply broaden existing film service on the local campus.

Before leaving the subject of TV, we may mention that some stations are holding up expensive conversions to color and more elaborate installations for film reproduction of programs in anticipation of TV tape. Routine taping of TV programs is now commercially feasible and is expected to be standard operating procedure for educational agencies in two to five years.

Handled in a manner identical with that of the magnetic recording of sound on wire, tape, or coated film, the new TV tape process will reduce costs tremendously, ease editing, and provide the marvel of electronic erasure as desired without loss. A fairly reputable collection of TV tapes for teaching and individual study may be the norm in many colleges and universities in a few years. Looking toward the use of small industrial cameras, similar to those described earlier, and low-cost reproducing equipment, one can foresee the possibility, for example, in education or social studies, of undertaking regular international exchange of classroom-made TV tapes without solving complex problems of production, meeting impossible costs, or other problems. This practice is not too far away in progressive undergraduate instruction—a decade at most.

LIBRARY PRINCIPLES

As suggested previously, the speaker believes that the major determinants of the place of newer media in American colleges and universities have relatively little to do with their physical aspects, psychological benefits, or disadvantages. The key problems are more mundane, and they are problems very familiar to librarians: locating reputable and sufficient sources of material; finding adequate tools for selection; establishing means for satisfactory processing; procuring adequate storage space and facilities for use and distribution; a knowledgeable faculty; and student readiness to make effective use of the materials available. There is nothing new about any of these problems. The acceptance of campus-wide responsibility of the college library to work toward their solution is usual, or, at least, is the recommended professional practice. Librarians who are most disturbed by the prospect of handling newer media base their opposition primarily on previous adverse experience with amateurish or poorly produced materials or on maintenance and storage problems, poor budgetary prospects, the distribution of audio-visual equipment, the need to discover an interested and trained staff, fears for the displacement of print, resentment of blatant and superficial promotional ventures which have sought an expanding field of support for use of motion pictures, filmstrips, etc., and perhaps a personal sense of inadequacy in facing the increased responsibility. In the predicament of having to "take audio-visual anyhow," too many librarians have done about the only thing which seemed to them possible under the circumstances. They have studied the operations of nonlibrary audio-visual departments, hired someone interested primarily in the newer media, whether a librarian or not, and set up shop—an audio-visual shop, imitating, to the last minute detail, their nonlibrary counterparts and making certain in the process that the operation does not get too "big for its boots" or become "a tail which wags the dog." The result of such administrative arrangements is constant fear and protective measures taken by the librarian, frustration and circumventive extra-legal procedures inaugurated by the audio-visual specialist, generally poor selection of materials in subject fields, and, in short, internecine warfare or, at best, an armed, competitive truce. If this picture seems incredible, or at least distorted, to some, I would like to assure you that it is a mirror image of many situations.

Tragically, the situation need not exist at all. Whether on a large university or small college campus, observance of a few general principles will resolve most problems of library planning for audio-visual administration. Architectural solutions to seeming difficulties of arrangement will be seen easily after acceptance of these aims. The first principle follows: Work for *maximum decentralization of responsibility for materials selection and counseling* according to subject departmentalization or divisional or broad subject areas. In serving an undergraduate program particularly, the librarian must play an active participating role in curriculum-planning groups and in some instances may be a formal, as well as informal, member of the teaching faculty. Only librarians with strong subject backgrounds or area interests can really be expected to give intelligent counsel regarding the potential contribution of a new set of slides, its relationship to other materials, gaps in the collection, etc., or talk intelligently about a new film or recording in a special subject field. An audio-visual generalist will usually be familiar with teaching methods and may give more valuable advice than uninterested librarians, but he can never become a specialist in all fields of knowledge simultaneously. Therefore, to repeat: intensive cross-media subject preparation is required to weigh levels and the potential contribution to learning of specific materials and to achieve a blend of recommendations which may achieve a given educational objective.

A second principle calls for *maximum decentralization of materials and equipment for preview and study in the library*. In presenting this idea, it is assumed that each academic department will have ready access to equipment for its own use in the classroom. With open shelves and the general trend toward new and more informal furniture arrangements, it is no longer difficult to house physically, in the same area and by subject, materials having several different forms. In those relatively few situations where temperature and moisture are important for preservation (almost an anachronism in the library buildings of today with air conditioning, general use of acetate film, etc.) a central area, comparable to the core stack area, having direct means of access to important functional or subject library departments, may be the solution. With enough pairs of earphones, hooded screens, and short-focal-length lenses, it is now physically possible and, in fact, desirable to offer individual or small group preview facilities in or directly adjacent to reading areas. Larger groups, discussion sections, or classes might meet in a small centrally located auditorium.

A third general principle suggests *maximum centralization of audio-visual equipment* and repair facilities, i.e., purchasing, distribution, and maintenance of equipment, film inspection and repairs, equipment booking, and other technical and clerical operations. Such functions are easily departmentalized and can be administered satisfactorily by technically trained nonprofessional personnel. The arrangement would not bar semipermanent loan of projectors, tape recorders, or other devices to academic departments as needed or their use in the library. They would, however, insure maximum utilization of expensive equipment, consistent observance of a suitable purchasing policy, responsible maintenance and repairs. Perhaps an extra word of caution is in order here. For years the physical plant or maintenance departments of some universities have tried to maintain a stranglehold on distribution and use of audiovisual equipment. Such practice means eventual warfare, occasional classroom

lockouts by union projectionists, the inevitable presence in the class or meeting room of persons not generally interested in the proceedings, and a continuing bitterly jealous struggle for prestige and funds. Ultimately, the chief librarian must be responsible for the purchase and distribution of equipment as well as materials if both are to be readily available and used efficiently.

Principle No. 4 may not always apply fully to research collections. But, on college levels, *central acquisition, processing, and a unified catalog* are mandatory. The unified catalog, of course, implements a cross-media subject approach by the librarian, student, or teacher and works quite well in smaller libraries. In larger institutions the gross physical size of the catalog and the necessity of looking through hundreds of cards to find any particular title would suggest division by form, but actual location of the trays on neighboring pedestals. The exact size at which a unified catalog becomes unmanageable (and let us assume the use of colored cards to indicate types of material) is a figure I would very much like to discover, if it is not already known.

My fifth and last principle relates to production of new materials. It requires a brief introduction. In some situations, circumstances will dictate the location of facilities for production of TV and radio programs, charts, graphic materials, and the like in the library, and certainly librarians should be ready to produce good materials for library orientation, publicity, and public relations. Photoduplication, microphotography, and disk and tape recorders are essential to perpetuate the life of existing materials or to record significant voices and events for future reference and teaching. The college librarian planning a new building will quite wisely incorporate in his first drawings space and facilities for studios to implement musical, film, or other programs to be broadcast in or out of the library. However, at least a tentative line should be drawn somewhere. I draw my line in this way. The library should not (save for duplication, transformation of existing materials, or recording of significant events) accept primary responsibility for original creative production of new materials. In my opinion, the college or university press, art service, photographic laboratory, and the production units of other media should be administered separately. Proximity to the library is, of course, highly desirable, but administrative supervision and control may or may not prove fortunate. John Moriarty, at Purdue, has such a dual span of responsibility, and there must be occasions when he finds it troublesome. In short, I believe it is generally advisable to *separate distribution from production responsibilities* for the newer media.

The five principles stated above summarize some personal thinking about the library's role in the field of nonprint or audio-visual materials. Their acceptance implies a number of additional responsibilities and difficulties which we have glossed over lightly thus far: for example, a continuing need for actively training members of the college community to make effective use of materials and equipment; the need for book-oriented subject librarians to learn to know and appreciate the values of new materials and keep pace with the results of new production, techniques of use, etc.; a need to locate and make a continuing search for new sources of information about audio-visual materials in a literature which, bibliographically

speaking (to put it mildly, despite very noble efforts of many professional library and audio-visual groups to create order), is still chaotic; the need to help bring to completion projects for evaluation (such as those conducted by the Educational Film Library Association); production of union lists (such as those produced by the three universities of Washington, a list of free films prepared by the Louisiana State Library, and a guide to 16-mm. nontheatrical films in Illinois); the necessity of insuring that additions of new materials and equipment to the library bring with them new funds, more space, and a larger staff (some librarians argue pragmatically that existence of two administrative units will draw more college funds for materials than one, a point not without some justice, despite its uneconomic aspects); etc.

If these worries are not sufficient, the interested librarian might be wise to take sides soon in a growing fight to professionalize the audio-visual field as such through certification. If this movement is not stopped, some librarians will find themselves automatically barred by definitions in state laws, through failure to meet prescribed educational standards, from provision of any nonprint services. (I hope no one at this conference finds the possibility attractive.) The situation could become embarrassing, especially in state-supported schools. Most libraries are already in the business, one way or another, with slides, photographs, sketches, and reproductions in the art collection, recordings in music, libraries, microfilm and microcards in the reference room, exhibits in the corridors and, in short, almost everything but films, filmstrips, models, and equipment.

Another facet of the library's responsibility for newer media attaches to eventual reference, research, and archival functions. The functions may not yet be too important to the undergraduate program, nor have the real needs or possibilities been thoroughly explored as yet. A forthcoming monograph to be published by A.C.R.L. will touch lightly on the subject, if I can locate the information.

The librarian's perennial problem of finding suitable personnel is obviously related to the philosophy and conduct of library education. At the present time, library-school faculties are doing little enough to prepare students for acceptance of general professional responsibilities, let alone meeting the prescriptions implied above. A cross-media approach and the need for audio-visual training are accepted in theory by many schools. But in only a few are real efforts being made to educate for realization of this theory in practice. The unusual training opportunities offered by the library schools of Florida State University, Indiana, and the University of Illinois, as reported at the American Library Association midwinter meeting in 1954 and issued as "Proceedings of a Pre-conference Workshop on Audio-visual Materials and Library Education," are encouraging. In this same vein, the speaker is looking forward to Irving Lieberman's comprehensive report on the subject to be published during the coming summer. Financed by a grant of $20,000 from the Carnegie Corporation, Lieberman has studied intensively the needs for, and methods of achieving, a satisfactory approach to training in librarianship for effective handling and use of the newer media.

CONCLUSION

Just one year ago, on June 19, Dr. Raynard C. Swank, director of libraries at Stanford University and a long-time advocate of audio-visual services in libraries, delivered an address before the ALA preconference Audio-Visual Workshop held at the University of Southern California. Entitled "Sight and Sound in the World of Books," this address has since been published in the *Library Journal*. It represents the first and only time I have heard, and later read with even greater pleasure, the words of a prominent university librarian advocating principles similar to the views urged today. The address was outstanding (I think that is true regardless of personal agreement), and I can think of no better way to conclude this paper than by quoting several excerpts from Dr. Swank's own closing paragraphs:

Audio-visual materials are not a single, separate type of medium, but a wide variety of media serving all kinds of purposes. These media . . . are more closely related functionally to books that serve the same purposes than to each other. Thus a recording of Robert Frost reciting his own verses is more akin to the printed text of those verses than to a motion-picture film on the rearing of children. There is a lesson in this for us, who think of ourselves as audio-visual specialists, prepare courses for audio-visual instruction, and attend audio-visual workshops. We are not a separate profession, and we ought not isolate ourselves or our work. . . .

We should not permit an isolated audio-visual library to arise within the library or anywhere else, unless unavoidable circumstances, such as the nature of a library building, dictate a separate arrangement. . . .

If there is any unity in the audio-visual field, it derives from the gadgetry, the mechanical appurtenances, necessary to the use of most audio-visual materials. I think we should minimize this aspect of the work as much as possible, keep it out of sight. The less conscious our readers are of the apparatus, the better. We give our readers not wax, not phonographs, but the spoken word—the poem, the story, the drama told aloud. We give them not film, not projectors and beaded screens, but the vision of life recreated for their pleasure and understanding. These are the things that books are made of too, and therein lies real unity.

When sight and sound are fully accepted in the world of books, when the unity of content is fully recognized, we will have better libraries, better readers, and better people.

BIBLIOGRAPHY

A.C.R.L. COMMITTEE ON AUDIO-VISUAL WORK. "Audio-visual Services in Colleges and Universities in the United States." Unpublished typescript. Tucson: The Committee, May, 1953.

DAVIES, DAVID W. "Audio-visual Materials," *Library Buildings For Library Service: Papers Presented before the Library Institute at the University of Chicago, August 5–10, 1946*, Pp. 86–93. Chicago: American Library Association, 1947.

DE KIEFFER, ROBERT E. (ed.). "The Utilization of Audio-visual Services in General Education," *Proceedings of the Third Stephens College Conference on Effective Utilization of Audio-visual Materials in College Teaching, April 18–20, 1951*. Columbia, Mo.: Stephens College, 1951.

HARCLEROAD, FRED F., and ALLEN, W. H. (eds.). *Audio-visual Administration*. Dubuque, Iowa: Wm. C. Brown Co., 1951.

HOCKING, ELTON. "The Power of Babel," *Educational Screen*, XXX (December, 1951), 400–401.

KINDER, JAMES S. "Audio-visual Research: Where To Find It," *Audio-visual Communication Review*, I (fall, 1953), 234–41.

LARSON, LAWRENCE C., and RUNDAN, CHARITY E. (eds.). *Bibliography of Research in Audio-visual Education and Mass Media, 1930–1950*. Bloomington: Indiana University, Audio-Visual Center, 1950.

McCLUSKY, FREDERICK D. *The A-V Bibliography*. Dubuque, Iowa: Wm. C. Brown Co., 1950.

"Proceedings of a Pre-conference Workshop on Audio-visual Materials and Library Education, Chicago, Illinois, February 1, 1954." (Mimeographed.)

SCHWARTZ, J. C. *Evaluative Criteria for an Audio-visual Instruction Program*. Dubuque, Iowa: Wm. C. Brown Co., 1950.

SWANK, RAYNARD C. "Sight and Sound in the World of Books," *Library Journal*, LXXVIII (September 15, 1953), 1459–64.

FINANCE AND THE COLLEGE LIBRARY

REUBEN FRODIN

THIS is a melancholy subject to which I have been summoned. The college or university librarian today is rarely the object of his master's affection. President John D. Millett, of Miami University, when he was a professor surveying the problems of financing higher education, reports he found that librarians drew more derogatory language from presidential pews than did other seals which needed feeding. I am reminded of a line from an English popular song quoted somewhere by George Orwell: "He's dead, but he won't lie down."

Is this the librarian I see before me: the person across the campus living in the building designed by an architect itching to do an interurban railway station, presiding over a staff of faithful but hungry loafers, and dealing with a nonfungible commodity which wants companionship only too fast? The librarian is unpopular in the front office today because the library is a fixed expense without apparent glamour. The president is tempted to paraphrase Gertrude Stein and say a book is a book is a book. He may also subscribe, unconsciously to be sure, to Miss Stein's observation: "Americans do not need a narrative of every day of any day, they have nothing to tell of the living of every moment in a daily living, they have nothing to say of living every day that makes it be a really soothing thing to say."[1]

Now the librarian, he is different. By training and temperament he has a respect for the book, and he lives in the

wonderful world of books. Miss Stein, writing in the less gaudy days before jet and TV, observed: "Think of the American life as it is lived, they all move so much even when they stay still and they do very often stay still they all move so much."[2] The librarian, of course, needs money to stay still, and that is the root of the problem.

When I accepted the responsibility for preparing this paper, I had a gnawing suspicion that I was expected to come up with an answer to one of two questions. These questions are: "How can we find the funds which are necessary to support a college library?" and "How do we cut down the support of the college library?" You may say, and with reason, that such a simple approach to a subject so exhaustively covered in the professional literature is silly. And you are right. You may also say there is no answer to the first question, and the second query belongs in a class with the celebrated "When did you stop beating your wife?" Again, you would be right. At the time I agreed to write this paper I was finishing my five-year stint as secretary of the Midwest Inter-Library Corporation—which had found funds to build and maintain a library's library for the great research institutions of the region. I had had an administrative hand in the building, within four years, of a staff and a book collection of 60,000 volumes for a new liberal arts college and was at work on the building plans for the entire college—including the library structure. I had recommended and seen carried to

[1] Gertrude Stein, *Narration* (Chicago: University of Chicago Press, 1935), p. 5.

[2] *Ibid.*, p. 11.

100

completion a detailed survey of the libraries and the personnel problems of the twenty-seven colleges and institutes of State University of New York. I had sat, for more than a year, with the Regents' Committee on Integration of College and University Library Resources in New York State. I cite these activities, not to establish myself as an expert, but to concede freely that there are no simple and dust-proof answers to those two questions: (1) How can we find the funds which are necessary to support a college library? and (2) How do we cut down the support of the college library?

Let it be said here and now: read the professional literature on the subject of the college library. It is exhaustive, and at times exhausting. It has the meat and potatoes of your job on the plate, but do not think that you will always get a bigger meal ticket by sticking the pile of books on administering the college library on the desk of your president. The statistics in *College and Research Libraries* are good. Be represented therein, study and analyze the statistics; but do not rely on them too much, because you can find authorities pro and con on the question of the validity of "per student operating expense" and "ratio of library expense to total expense" as surefire arguments with the front office. Before the war McCrum *et al.* reported that $25 per student was the minimum; in November, 1951, Moran and Tolman[3] suggested the figure of $50 per student and reported that fewer than 10 per cent of the colleges they had surveyed spent that much for their libraries. And yet, if you picked a group of libraries that you would like to emulate, as I did, in preparing this paper, you would find that

[3] Virginia L. Moran and Mason Tolman, "College Library Study," *Library Journal*, LXXVI (1951), 1906–10.

the per student figures ran this way: $61, $67, $75, $85, $100, $39, and $81. These are for long-established private colleges, to be sure.

I am a firm believer in the discussion method of teaching, and if you admit before you start that it is often harder to ask the right questions that it is to answer them, we can proceed with a discussion. But since this has been billed as a lecture, you will have to bear with me while we roll the crystal dice without spots around a bit. First, let us throw out the two questions which have been gnawing me for the past few months and start afresh. Let us try the twenty-question approach.

1. Does the kind of educational institution make a difference in determining the cost and character of the library? The answer is, of course, Yes. And yet I have found that trustees and administrators have frequently—and I want to say, more often than not—failed to take into consideration the library when embarking on a new program or a new curriculum. I know of one institution with a small enrolment that proudly sets forth that it has seventeen different curriculums to offer. There is no doubt that such institutions—and there are a great many in the United States—cannot afford to support an adequate library.

Our New York Regents' Committee attempted a general answer to the question with this: The college library collection will be relatively simple or complex in direct relation to the diversity and level of its courses and to variation in teaching methods. It is submitted that the seventeen-curriculum college should have more books than a one-curriculum college. I use these numbers now somewhat figuratively to make another point. That is this: The institutions which have the simpler curriculum structure seem to have the best libraries. Do not the trustees and administrators of colleges which have widely expanded the scope of their offerings without attention to the implications for their libraries have something to answer for? In the matter of teaching methods in relation to libraries, a book might be written. It can only be suggested here that a course of study which relies on textbooks and lectures can perhaps do without too much of a library. And a course of study demanding that students purchase many books containing required readings may mean a smaller library than one in a college with an extensive honors program.

2. What is an adequate library? This is perhaps the most difficult of all questions, and yet by far the most interesting. The Regents' Committee wrestled long and hard with it, and, while the answer is not complete and will satisfy no one, here it is:[4]

As far as the book collection is concerned, each college should supply: (a) *required reading materials*, such as reserved books. (b) *recommended reading materials*. (c) *periodicals* needed to support the curriculum. In all these basic areas, it is recommended that only in emergencies should borrowing from another library be considered. (d) *materials for special studies and honors work*. Here again the college library should supply the basic material; borrowing should be limited to additional materials which show little prospects of continued usefulness in the college library. (e) *Some general, cultural, recreational reading*, chosen not because it relates to the curriculum but because the items are regarded as desirable in content and in quality of

[4] *A Plan for Meeting College Library Problems: A Report of the Regents' Committee on Integration of College and University Library Resources in New York State* (Albany: State Education Department, 1954), pp. 8–9.

presentation for college readers. (f) *Some materials for faculty members*. This is one of the hardest areas to define and will vary from college to college. Certainly, each college should supply its faculty with some materials on higher education, for instance. Many colleges will feel that even though few students are skilled enough to read complex materials in certain languages, the fact that the most pertinent information on some subjects appears in foreign books and periodicals which the faculty can read necessitates their purchase. In general, perhaps it is safe to say that such material which "plays back" into the quality of the teaching should be bought whenever possible. Material used by faculty members in research which is less directly related to their teaching should be bought when the *prospects of its continued usefulness seem to merit the expenditure*. (g) *Materials to support special curricula* (i.e., nursing, religious, ceramics, music, law, military, naval, fashion, etc.). (h) *College archives and history; some local materials*. (i) *Pamphlets, pictures, clippings, and other ephemera*. (j) *Basic references and bibliographic tools*, but not every edition of each publication.

We then went on to list kinds of material which are found in a university library, which may be needed by a college but are generally outside its means: (a) complete files of important periodicals; (b) major reference books of all types; (c) rare or expensive books; (d) background books; (e) government publications; (f) college and university catalogs, retrospective files; (g) theses and dissertations; (h) corporation and other reports; (i) lesser works of well-known writers; (j) duplicates of books outdated that should be weeded from college libraries; (k) bibliography; (l) library literature; (m) developing fields that are too new to warrant college acquisitions.

You may say that this is all well and good, but where does that leave us? Our attempt, like mine herein, is to assist in the construction of criteria which can be used in measuring the adequacy of the college library. I have already suggested per student expenditures, the character of the college program, the methods of teaching, and now two checklists: (a) a list of classes of materials which ought to be in the college library and (b) another list of kinds of things that should be available through another institution or other institutions.

3. Is the size of the college important? In my opinion it is critical. Whether a college has 200, 400, 600, 800, 1,000, or more students is a major factor in approaching the problem of the adequacy of the library. And, of course, its cost. Two of the libraries somewhat cryptically referred to earlier in this paper reported per student expenditures for library purposes of $39 and $85. The former has a student body of more than 1,200 and the latter a few under 600. They both seem to me to be good libraries, and each offers adequate services to its student body. I have not examined their book collections, but my impression is that they are equally good. I am not, of course, talking about special collections or rare books—those crown jewels which librarians fortunate to have wealthy alumni with bibliophilic instincts use to draw more jewels. I was talking of size; and I must add that librarians cannot be asked to determine the size of the college. They can tell their administrators, however, that two colleges of similar age and curriculum, one with 375 students and the other with 850, and each spending $33 per student, will probably have rather different libraries. And yet, it is

submitted, these two colleges probably ought to have similar book collections.

4. What standards of service should be expected of the library? You may have felt, by the emphasis devoted so far to book collections, that I have forgotten service. On the contrary, I am well aware that in a college library 60–70 per cent of today's library budget will go for salaries and hourly wages. I am well aware that the gross amount for personal services has increased a great deal in the last fifteen years. The private colleges in some areas of the country shake their fists at the state institutions and blame them for the lack of personnel and the high cost of it. The problem is, of course, much more complicated. At the risk of oversimplification, I can only suggest that the wages paid to stenographic help by big business in urban centers has much more to do with library clerical wages than any other factor; this, in turn, will tend to dictate civil service wages in the states; and the familiar results follow.

If this seems unresponsive to the question, forgive me. Remember what I said about asking the right questions. But money for personal services and standards of service are very much at the heart of our problem. The college library is, in the first place, a place for books and readers. It may be a study hall. It may be a lounge. It may have audio-visual materials, with galleries and listening booths. It has workrooms for a staff, for ordering and receiving and cataloging, and so forth. It takes dollars to run a library; this is obvious. But it is up to the administrator to reach agreement with the faculty, the library staff, and (in effect) the students as to what services are to be offered. It is hard, but it is not an impossible job. There should be some agreement about the adequacy of the present collection, based on studies which the faculty should be asked to make first, then a check and an analysis by the library of such studies; next, there should be some agreement on the rate of acquisitions. Periodicals. Binding. Microfilm readers. Microfilm. And so forth. The librarian can estimate what this will cost to handle if the doors were never opened to students. Then, if there are funds left, he can figure out how long he wants to keep the building open, and if architecture permits, how few people he will need at off-peak hours. It will be decided that reference work is good or bad and, assuming it is good, how much he can afford. But I will not proceed any further: there is no formula to give the president of your institution as to standards of library service. You can help him, but he has to decide. Moran and Tolman reported median salaries of full-time subprofessional and clerical workers in the libraries they studied at $1,950 per year, and the median for order librarians in 54 institutions at $1,700. When an operating vice-president of one of our American steamship companies told me recently that the room steward—with eight cabins to care for—on the liner on which he had crossed the Atlantic netted considerably in excess of $8,000 per year, I was reminded of the fact that the highest salary of a college librarian reported to Moran and Tolman was $7,500.

5. Are books and personnel the only problems which the college library faces? No. If one can generalize from the results of a survey made for the Regents' inquiry in New York State, space is the major problem. Fourteen colleges out of 42 reported that they had zero years to go before exhaustion of their shelf space. Another 17 reported that they had from one to five years left, and the remaining 11 said that they had more than five years of shelf "life." The "potential discards" that these libraries reported—to to a nonexistent storage center or to the waste basket—would not, in my opinion, make an appreciable difference in their space problems.

This observation leads me to several more, which serve to emphasize some of the difficulties, with suggestions frequently made about "voluntary co-operation among libraries." In the course of the development during the last five years of the great storehouse of little-used research materials in the Midwest Inter-Library Center, the director and the representatives of the co-operating libraries have discussed the possible services of the Center for college libraries. The conclusions reached seemed to be these: (a) The book collection of the Center would be of no more or no less benefit to a faculty member of a college than it would if he were a scholar at a university; (b) the collection would not supplement the college collection in the way a university library would; (c) in the matter of periodicals, for example, there was a great difference between the kind of periodicals which universities would share among themselves through the Center and the kind of periodicals which colleges might share; and (d) deposits which might afford space relief (but probably not very much) could be considered if they fell into categories laid out by the Center. It was further felt among the librarians who discussed the matter that, while co-operative programs among college libraries remain a line of approach which must be studied, there were yet no general guides to follow. The Hampshire Inter-Library Center program should and will be followed with interest. Proximity and available space in one of the three libraries involved has permitted an auspicious start of the program.

In the early deliberations of the Regents' Committee it was quite clear to most of the members that the problems of New York State's largest research libraries (the New York Public Library, the Columbia University libraries, the Cornell University libraries, and the New York State Library in Albany, with total resources of approximately 10,000,-000 items) were quite different from those of, say, forty college libraries reporting annual acquisitions of under 3,000 volumes.

This is not the occasion for a discussion of the problems of the research libraries or for a report on the progress of the Regents' Committee in its discussions of those problems. It may be said, however, that the committee did recommend that the New York State Library should be strengthened to serve as a library's library for the colleges of the state. It also recommended that the state library publish a short-title catalog by the punched-card method, with annual supplements, which would greatly facilitate use of the library at a distance. To some extent, the state library, with its million volumes and nearly two million pamphlets, manuscripts, and maps, has been serving the whole state for years in various fields. It was felt by the committee that the services could be improved so that the state library would be able "to supply materials and services which, though they may be out of reach for separate colleges if each tries to supply them at home, will prove to be economical, efficient, and highly beneficial if offered by one center to all." The categories in which it was hoped that the state library would supplement the college collections, as suggested by the committee, are essentially the thirteen enumerated previously as those in which a college occasionally needs material but for which it has to go

to a university or research library. Since the state library already contains much that will meet the extraordinary needs of the colleges, the proposals seemed to have practical merit.

I realize full well that there may be no other state library which can be put in a position, with any reasonable expenditure of funds, to augment the collections of colleges in its state. Nor do I suggest for one minute that the proposals in New York will solve all college-library problems, least of all the space problem.

6. Can college libraries economize? "Nobody, but nobody, undersells Gimbels" is the way the advertisement of a well-publicized competitor of Macy's reads. Nobody, but nobody, knows the answer to this question. Millett, in his *Financing Higher Education in the United States*, states that "the librarian profession as such puts little emphasis on economy."[5] In a letter to a librarian who challenged this statement, Millett reported that this was a generalization made on the basis of his interviews with presidents and deans all over the country. I feel after rereading Millett and after surveying the materials which have shaped this paper that it would be wrong to apply this generalization to the efforts of *college* librarians; and by saying this I am not entering into a consideration of the relevance to university librarians or the problems of university and research libraries. My feeling is—and this is shared by all university librarians with whom I discussed the matter—that Millett did not distinguish sufficiently between the different sets of problems faced by the college libraries and by the research libraries. For the purposes of discussion, therefore, it is submitted that one cannot study the statistics of the very large

[5] (New York: Columbia University Press, 1952), p. 123.

number of college libraries reporting expenditures of less than $30,000 per year and feel that there is much room for economy. You cannot look at any of the recent surveys of salaries in the college libraries—and I have referred to one above—and suggest that the staffs are overpaid.

It may be that there are colleges that should not remain in business today because they do not have the dollar resources; but it would be unfair, I believe, to say that economy in libraries is a real source for financial savings. This may be an appropriate place to record that, in connection with the Regents' Committee recommendations for the New York State colleges, it was recommended that a college-library consultant be placed on the staff of the state library to help college libraries (upon request) and act to promote co-operation between them and the state library. It was unanimously felt by the librarians that such a person would be of assistance to the colleges in many areas, not the least of which might be in bringing a reasonably objective view of local library problems to the attention of the college president.

7. Are the library problems in the public and private colleges the same, or are they different? Some of the problems are different, but many are the same. It should be mentioned that problems have different aspects in various parts of the nation. Taking again the distinction between research and college libraries as one not difficult for librarians to accept, although budget officers, legislators, some trustees, and the public may not grasp the difference easily, we may try a few generalizations. Money is just as hard to get for the libraries of public colleges as it is for the nonpublic. And I am not attempting to pass judgment in any way on the libraries of Brooklyn College

and Hunter College in New York City when I point out that for 25,000 students between them they struggle to get $14 per student for their libraries. Look at the expenditures for the libraries of the teachers' colleges in several states and put the same tests that you put to other college libraries. These institutions are producing many thousands of college graduates each year. The library resources and reading space and attendant services are not what they should be. Be assured that prying money out of budget officers and legislators in many states is just as difficult as is squeezing the lemon peel in many presidents' offices in the private colleges. The solution of the problem of the adequacy of the libraries is different in practically every instance. In many states the rationalization of the problem of its colleges is probably impossible. Historical accidents, because of political decisions or compromises made years ago, mean, in a few words, that some states have to buy ten sets of the *Encyclopaedia Britannica* rather than one or two.

8. As a practical matter, what should the college librarian do? The finances of the college library are linked to the financial position of the college; the library should have a fair share of the operating budget. It is the librarian's responsibility to relate his needs to the instructional program of the college and to present these needs realistically to his president. The librarian should take the initiative, in approaches suggested above in this paper, in determining the scope of the collection and level of services of the library appropriate to the financial position of the college. The final decisions and the ultimate responsibility, however, are not his. He should take the lead in "weeding" and should secure faculty participation, through an interested library

committee, in a series of "alternative plans" for the book collection. He should follow and co-operate in any feasible plan of co-operation with other college libraries, realizing—to point up an obvious, yet often forgotten, matter—that co-operation usually requires much more giving than getting.

In cutting the cloth of the library to fit the college, there is always one thought to keep the tailor happy. No matter how little money is made available for books, it is always possible to buy good books. The interest perennially shown in the Sunday-supplement question: "What ten books would you take with you if you were going to be cast on a desert island?" is not without significance to the college librarian. Call this the "great-book" theory of the library if you wish. It is submitted that whether you have money for 300 books a year, 1,000 books, or 3,000, it is possible to purchase 300, 1,000, or 3,000 books which college students should have the opportunity to read—and which it would be intellectually profitable for them to read. I would say the same to those librarians—or to those teachers whose responsibility is for a few shelves of books—if they can buy only 50 or 100 books. If every student reads 50 good, significant, or great books per year, he has a better chance at an education than if he does not. This again brings us up against the question of the objectives of college education and of the means used in a particular instance to attain them.

The college librarian is a bookman. He is a physical guardian of books and, one can hope, in nearly every instance the guardian of the more important rather than the less important ones. He can provide a place in which the student can be started upon the intellectual road which is the freedom of the mind, because through books and talking with himself, with his teacher, and with his fellow-students, the student may rightfully earn his place in the intellectual community. Freedom of the mind is not a state easily obtained, nor is it a condition immune from attack. Pressures which squeeze or push to the wall those with original or heretical thought; crude or sophisticated weapons which terrorize opinion—these are the forces, as Samuel Eliot Morison has recently said, that "encourage timidity among teachers and researchers and an ugly anti-intellectualism among the people." The harm to American institutions can be great.

The role of the librarian is clear. He is humble and not smug. He is, in the best sense of the word, the guardian of the books and what is in them. He participates in the work of the college, the work which makes it possible, through the transmission of words and ideas, to create in these young men and young women who have the privilege and the right to read freely and widely a sense of participation in the intellectual community and to make it possible for them to assume the burden of furthering and bettering our free society. The road is long and hard, but it is paved with good books.

SOME PROBLEMS IN COLLEGE LIBRARIANSHIP

HERMAN H. FUSSLER

IT IS not the purpose of the remarks that follow to summarize, abstract, or recapitulate the papers that have been presented to this conference. Instead, it is my intention to try to isolate and point to a few of the major problems, trends, or observations that have been mentioned by the speakers in their separate analyses of various aspects of the college library.

First, I have asked myself whether, out of the papers that have been presented, there has emerged a picture of the college library in operation that is markedly different from the rather clear and definitive picture already given us by Branscomb, Lyle, Randall, L. R. Wilson, and other writers on the subject. It seems to me that the answer to this question must be No, if we limit our examination to the broad outlines of the college library as a social structure. In these terms the college library is doing what these authors have told us it is doing, and it is doing these things in approximately the ways in which they, a decade or more ago, described.

Similarly, if the question were asked, "Have the papers of the conference produced a unified, unambiguous, and definitive statement of the function of the library in the modern college?" I would also, I believe, answer, No. I would hastily add that such a statement was not anticipated from a conference which has as its primary purpose the presentation of ideas, suggestions, trends, and problems. "What then," you may ask, "have we accomplished?" It seems to me that we have reaffirmed our acceptance of a rather broad body of procedures, principles, and theories relating to the college library—which is a desirable thing to do from time to time with social institutions. We have similarly reaffirmed the existence of basic questions for which we do not have the data for answers, and, perhaps more significantly, we have recognized certain trends and directions in which the college library has moved or is very likely to move if it is to be successful in fulfilling its functions. We have also recognized a number of important difficulties that may affect the operations, the purposes, and the successful adaptation of the college library to the needs of the college. Thus, while little that is dramatically new has been stated, some old problems have been restated with greater clarity and insight, and new directions have been set forth for our guidance. These are not negligible accomplishments if we are able to make use of them.

It seems to me that one of the most pervasive elements of the conference has been the underlying sense of critical urgency attached to the values of a liberal education in modern life. While most of us have always believed in the values of a liberal education, there is an implicit recognition in much that has been said during this conference that, unless we are able to transmit such values to a very substantial part of our population, those parts of our civilization that free men must hold most dear are in actual danger of extinction. We are at last coming to recognize that a knowledge of science alone will not make us free men, nor will skill in the pursuit of wealth—though we need not deprecate either. It is now evident that even if we succeed in inculcating those liberal attitudes of mind that are necessary to nurture and sustain a truly democratic society, we still may see it perish because of external forces. Yet it must be equally clear that unless we can transmit an understanding of and a conviction in the liberal traditions, a democratic society will have no chance at all for survival. As President Davidson has succinctly stated, our judgments must be based on intellectual rather than emotional responses.

Because of these and other considerations, the conference speakers seem to be in full agreement concerning the importance of a liberal education and the fact that the liberal arts college must play a major role in providing our citizens with such an education. This task of the college is made even more difficult, since apparently it must also accept a considerable part of the burden of molding character and attitudes that were once largely shaped within the family and the church. While these findings of the conference can hardly claim to be new or unusual, they do carry a growing sense of urgency and reality.

The papers leave no doubt that good books and good libraries are absolutely essential elements in the provision of a liberal education. The necessity for the library as a direct service agency of the curriculum has been recognized and commented on rather specifically. The speakers are much less specific, however, in describing the processes through which the library discharges this burden. Some of these service functions have been described very clearly—required reading, for example—and the librarian is advised that some methods are better than others. As an illustration, our speakers

make it clear that if we have been keeping the purse strings drawn very tightly for the purchase of duplicate copies of books required in course work, we may be well advised to relax them a bit, in order to make the library a more effective instrument in the instructional program, which must take precedence over all other elements in the college library's operations and services.

But in pointing to the more specific aspects of these service relationships—i.e., reserve reading, sources of information for term papers, etc.—there are explicit and implicit observations that the college library has a wider and more diffuse function that it must fill—though we should note that the speakers have been rather emphatic in limiting this role to the needs of the local institution. This function, as I say, is not described with precision but appears to satisfy a number of underlying concepts. For example, the reading of good books, within reason, is thought to be a good thing, and therefore it ought to be encouraged—within reason. Arragon tells us that a primary function of the library is to facilitate the self-education of the student, while Gwynn argues that a thorough understanding of and skill in the use of a library is itself one of the liberal arts in modern society. Gwynn goes on to suggest that if college students are not able to use a college and, particularly, a university library, we should change the students, not the library. In the ideal university library there is a great deal to be said for this; but we should recognize parenthetically that the dispersion and other problems of housing and using the very large university library may defeat the college student physically and emotionally long before he is defeated intellectually.

It is my view that our speakers are

less precise about these things for two reasons. While there is agreement that a liberal education must be made an essential part of our society, there is anything but the medieval kind of agreement and understanding upon either the content or the methodology through which a liberal education can be conveyed. The second reason—and this seems to me also to be a second general finding of the conference—is that however the college library is used, it is essentially a humanistic device. We have all heard that well-worn phrase that the library is the laboratory of the humanities. I have always objected to this phrase because of the false dichotomy it seems to establish with the sciences, which need libraries just as much as do the humanities. Therefore, this is not what I mean in saying that the library is essentially a humanistic device. What I mean is that many of the characteristic uses and values of the college library are, speaking very broadly, humanistic in their patterns. Libraries have to do with the pursuit of ideas, an understanding of the human spirit, and the acquisition of a sufficient body of knowledge and experience to understand and cultivate the use of the intellectual processes. How can one determine the intellectual values to a student of reading a poem or the insight that comes from grasping a philosophical problem or the satisfactions of pursuing and finding factual information bearing upon a particular point of inquiry, not only in the humanities, but equally in the sciences—physical, biological, and social?

I would argue that McKeon's lucid and systematic description of the college-library book collection and its problems can lead to no other conclusion than that the entire college library is humanistic in these kinds of characteristic uses, and

the library must, in consequence, be at least partly appraised in humanistic terms. If you are willing to accept this view, then some of the other major problems that have been mentioned by various speakers may fall into sharper focus. Since the means by which a liberal education may best be accomplished are yet to be defined, it is hardly surprising that the precise methods by which the college library should be used or developed are yet to be precisely stated—and, indeed, may not yet be known.

The third general observation of the conference has to do primarily with a number of apparent inconsistencies or contradictions about librarians, the college library, and its services. Since it is evident that college libraries are as old as colleges and no one has yet admitted to a desire to do away with the libraries, why should we be uncertain about the position of the library and the librarian in the college? Are these uncertainties more than the librarian's usual searching (and public) examination of the actual role of the library as contrasted with some sought-for potential goal or ideal of service and, especially, use?

Here the answer seems to be Yes, it is more. One might infer from Davidson, Arragon, and McKeon that the college library is secure, that if it will only establish and maintain *rapport* with the faculty and the college administration, it will be made aware of the objectives it must meet and will find, or be shown, the ways in which it is best to meet them. The papers by Wilson and Parker, in particular, suggest that this *rapport* may be very difficult to establish and, even if established, may not lead directly to the best of all library worlds.

Let us begin, then, where we probably ought to begin, with the extent to which there is mutual understanding between the faculty and the libraries, and we must admit that some of the evidence is discouraging. Implicit in a number of papers and in our discussions is a suggestion that the librarian's concept of the function of the library may give the library a broader and more vital role in instruction than does the faculty's concept of the library. Wilson has reported studies showing that many librarians are skeptical of that most common device for mutual understanding, the library committee. It is generally agreed that the committees should have no administrative authority; yet many of the topics commonly considered by library committees, including some of those urged by the experts, are primarily administrative; other topics involve knowledge and information on which a standing committee may not be particularly competent; and the very fact that the committees are usually purely advisory and without legislative or policy-making powers may place the committee in so restrictive a situation as to make it a sterile instrument except under unusual circumstances. We ought to consider more carefully whether, if mutual understanding of needs and problems is our goal, as I am sure it must be, the library committee is the best device we can create for this purpose.

Wilson and Frodin both suggest that there are a number of other aspects of government, control, and finance that deserve more careful scrutiny and specification if we are to operate effectively and if we are to be understood. Along these lines are the statements attributed to Millett that are said to reflect the rather harsh views of a number of college and university presidents. If, in fact, the presidents are critical of their college and university librarians, is it for one or more of the following reasons: Have the librarians misconstrued the functions of the library and undertaken activities they should not have? Have the presidents a faulty conception of the needs and purposes of a library? Or is there something inherent in the library situation that creates hostility on the part of college and university administrators? I would answer that there may be something in each of these and more besides.

I assume, by definition, that we as librarians are all likable and approachable people and that therefore it is not as individuals that the presidents may find us troublesome. Furthermore, Millett's statements are so broad and sweeping that analysis is difficult. Thus it may be that the college librarians are all esteemed by their presidents and only the research and university librarians are in trouble. Let us, however, accept the criticisms at face value for the present and see what we can make of them. While Wilson shows us that there are counteropinions, we must recognize that even in the counterviews he presents there are potential sources for misunderstanding.

We should recognize what I think the conference has made very clear, namely, the position of the typical librarian by its very nature can be, and perhaps is even likely to be, a difficult one. On the one hand, he has the faculty, some of whom do not use books themselves and do not suggest that their students should use books. The librarian may recognize, often correctly, that both the faculty member and his students are missing something of real importance by their self-isolation from the library. A much larger number of faculty members are eager to build up as large and as inclusive a book collection as possible. They will always see that a book allocation is fully expended, but some will spend it more wisely than others. Suggestions of weeding, for example, to some of the faculty members, unless preceded by the most wise and tactful preparation, are likely to be received in shocked amazement. The librarian who proposes weeding runs the risk of being accused of not being a scholar or not being a bookman or, worse, of being deficient in both respects. I am exaggerating a bit, as you will see, but my point is this: by and large, a good faculty, as both McKeon and Arragon indicate, will today want access to more books and not fewer, and we are not likely to convince them easily that for every new book we add to our collections, one already there has become sufficiently obsolete or disused to withdraw. McKeon agrees, as most of us will if we think about it, that there must be an optimum size of collection for every institution at any point in time, but I am not entirely convinced that he really believes any college library has ever reached an optimum size, or ever will. However, even if we should all agree that every college library can be stabilized at some optimum level—a level that is almost certainly different for each college —we must admit that at the moment neither we nor our faculties know how to compute it.

A detailed examination of the statistics on expenditures of college libraries is not at all convincing yet that the library is actually getting more of the college or university budget as the years go by, but our fundamental position probably suggests this possibility, and it is easy to see that our requests for support seem to be insatiable. I am sure that the needs of every other department in a college or university are probably insatiable also. The difference, however, is that their demands tend to be broken up into small bits and irregular pieces: a new professorship here, an assistantship there, a re-

furbished laboratory this year, a new wing next year. These needs, furthermore, can usually be presented in the context of very clear and specific gains for the college. But the library is not and must avoid being thought of as a competitor with other parts of the college for the available funds. The need of supporting the library must be made apparent to every part of the college.

For on the other side of the librarian stand the president and, beyond him, the trustees. They are harassed and busy men. Much of their time these days goes, not to educational planning and theory, but to budgeting and to trying to find the money to keep our colleges and universities from bankruptcy. This is not very pleasant work, though I suppose it must have its compensations. Thus it is the unusual president indeed who can face with any pleasure or satisfaction the librarian's calm announcement that no matter how large the book budget, the faculty will insist that it ought to be larger, and the larger it is, the sooner a new library or library stack addition will be required. The benefits of buying more serial titles this year than last may be much more difficult to demonstrate than the benefits of a new roof on the gym. And, unfortunately, we are never satisfied simply with the money for the new titles. I am afraid that our needs always appear to be progressive, for each of these new serial titles has to be bound, each cataloged, and shelf space found for them all, not only for this year but for every year thereafter. Then we go on to frighten our administrative officers by saying, "Once we have added these things to the library, it will always appear to be cheaper to leave them there than to take them out and discard them."

Now I think librarians are here partly taking the blame for the actions and pressures that originate not with them but with their faculties. If this assumption is true, part of the solution may rest in making it much clearer to the president than we have where the pressures come from and, more importantly, why. We must also make the consequences of unrestrained growth much clearer to our faculties than we have, and administrators and faculties alike must come to see that the common definitions of materials that are needed for a college are not yet adequate to describe in any finite terms the quantitative scope of a collection. We ought also to take much more seriously than we may have in the past the need for budgetary stability and stable size. We may not attain these goals, they may even be the wrong goals, but we cannot reject these matters merely because of a subjective or a traditional dislike for them. Let us genuinely try to find out whether there is an optimum size of college library. If there is such a thing, we should welcome it; if there is not, let us convince our colleagues that there is not.

The librarian's position is also difficult because he is, in a sense, unique in the academic structure. Nominally he takes his orders from the president, for he is, as librarian, part of the administrative academic structure; but, in fact, his actions must be determined principally by faculty needs and directions. The faculty cannot, as individuals, command the librarian, nor can the librarian command the faculty. Wilson suggests that the misunderstandings that can grow out of this situation may be minimized by a more rigorous written statement of responsibilities, relationships, and procedures than is customary in many colleges. Certainly, a general understanding of these matters between the president, the faculty, and the librarian is essential

to smooth and effective operations. Yet it must also be clear that a detailed code will not, and should not, spell out all possible relationships, and it cannot substitute for the librarian's professional ability, his understanding of his job and the needs of faculty members and students, and his personality and skill in communicating with his colleagues.

The able and competent librarian can be helped enormously in serving his college effectively if his president will see that the librarian is placed where he will be able to learn, without ambiguity, what the needs of the faculty actually are, and where he will have an opportunity to voice his views on the relationships between their expressed needs, plans, and desires and the resources of the library. It has been suggested that one way of doing this is to give the librarian faculty status and rank. I venture to say that academic status is probably essential but that it, without the other elements I have mentioned, will accomplish very little.

In the face of these rather difficult relationships and conflicting pressures for expansion of collections and service, on the one side, and efficiency, economy, and budgetary stability, on the other, let us admit that we may at times look a bit unappetizing to our presidents. I suggest that we can and should find better ways of demonstrating the values of a library and the ways in which it is used, that we must be sure our faculties and our presidents know why we have the problems that we do, for our problems must also be theirs by the very nature of a library.

In the face of these generalizations, the library salary structure as reported by Wilson is disturbing, not so much because of the low salaries themselves as because of the implications of the adverse differentials between the librarians' salaries and the other administrative and teaching salaries. We see ourselves as major academic, administrative officers, charged with the responsibility for building, maintaining, and operating the single most complex, most expensive, and most widely used instrument of learning and research within any academic institution—cyclotrons and ion accelerators not excepted—the library. If we can believe the statistics of the N.E.A. study, we must reach one of the following conclusions: (1) librarianship is a professional task comparable in its responsibilities and training requirements to those of the lower ranks of academic instruction or to the lower levels of academic administration, or (2) a substantial number of college librarianships are filled with persons who are not highly competent and their salaries are a reflection of their competence, or (3) librarians have been in such great supply that they could be appointed at lower salaries than their ranks would otherwise indicate. I am not prepared to accept any of these conclusions and can only observe that a variety of very basic problems and difficulties are implied in the salary comparisons given in Wilson's paper. It must be abundantly clear that we cannot recruit people of high quality or retain them unless we are prepared to pay them adequate salaries.

In his discussion of personnel, Parker questions whether the profession is recruiting enough of the right kind of people and whether the library schools are doing the best with what they have. He suggests that we may be slower than we should be to recruit from unconventional sources of personnel and that our training for such people may be overly technical. If we pursue Parker's line of reasoning somewhat further, even more serious questions can be asked. Implicit in his paper is the idea that we may be repelling those whom we should attract, that the college library can use any one of a number of different kinds of talent from fields or disciplines foreign to librarianship, and that the professional elements in the training of librarians may be mastered quickly by a mature person and, in any case, are subordinate to other kinds of experience or training. For the present, we should recognize that these are carefully stated questions or opinions rather than facts, but we would be ill-advised if we did not weigh and evaluate them in relation to some of the problems I have already described.

The college library is a dynamic structure. In its avoidance of a stereotyped or stylized pattern and its willingness to try new lines of attack and to scrutinize and appraise its successes and failures lies much of its strength. In two areas—the newer media of teaching and library buildings—the conference has made it clear that change—and change for the better—is here and that more change can confidently be expected. The college library with its books locked away behind an imposing façade of desks, clerks, and library apparatus and procedures is rapidly vanishing. Instead we can visualize, if we have not actually seen, a library that recognizes the intellectual and physiological habits and comforts of the individual student. The books are visible, the student is invited to wander among them and use them freely and easily. The lighting, instead of striving to copy the *torchères* of a medieval palace, now tries to provide comfortable light for reading. A recognition of the needs of small groups, the desire of many students for some element of privacy for concentrated effort, the special requirements of the faculty, all are bringing into these libraries of inviting color and warmth more students than ever before. The library apparatus is still there for those who want it and need it, but it is not so conspicuous as it used to be. And at least some of the students are there to work. They are discovering that the college library is not a cold and officious bureaucracy but a place in which work, if not downright attractive, is at least made as comfortable as possible. Adams carefully points out that in our desire to avoid the kind of strangulation which our buildings in the past have often subjected us to, we are now seeking structures of great flexibility. He urges us to recognize that we can, unless we are careful, sacrifice current efficiency and effectiveness in order to be able to adjust for future undefined needs that may never materialize. If we are to have good buildings, our need to know what happens in a library is not reduced by our growing ability to alter or change a library when change is indicated. It is evident that a library building ought to be both adaptable and flexible; but a building which is only adaptable and flexible is not necessarily a library.

In his turn, Stone disabuses us of the idea, if we still have it, that the printed book in stiff covers is all that the undergraduate needs if he is to learn effectively. The book, to a student unable to read music, is unlikely to convey much of the beauty of a symphony. I am sure, from what he says, that the undergraduate library in the years ahead must broaden its perspective and acquire and use nonbook materials whenever they are more efficient than the book or serve as helpful supplements to it. The organization of materials, whatever their form, along subject lines is an adaptation that we have made only slowly with books. We are urged not to repeat the error of segregating the newer media simply because we, as librarians, may find it convenient administratively; above all, we should understand that the library is not necessarily the only organization on the campus that has the right to use and administer these interesting and, in some ways, troublesome materials.

In summary, the conference has made it clear that, while we know a great deal about the college library, we still have a great deal to learn. The library as a direct service adjunct to the curriculum seems to be reasonably well understood. Yet even here there are clear gaps in our knowledge: we are aware that many students, even in direct, curriculum-related assignments, cannot make effective use of the library. We have yet to agree upon a pattern by which they can acquire such skill most effectively. But perhaps we should not be too alarmed by this, for it is only very recently that college authorities have become aware that a surprisingly large number of our college students cannot even read as well as they need to if they are to handle their course work satisfactorily.

It has been suggested that there are intangible values to be gained by a student's cultivating a use of the library that is over and beyond the direct requirements of his courses. Yet we know that few students make any considerable use of the library in this way. In our discussions of the papers, it has emerged that even the number of faculty members who understand and use the library widely—that is, beyond the immediate and very specific needs of their teaching and research—is likely to be very small. Actually, then, we must still find answers to parts of the question, "What should a college library be, and how should it be used?"

We are told that the book collection

must be high in quality, very carefully selected, and designed around the needs of the curriculum, the wide-ranging general cultural interests of students and faculty, and the research or informational needs of the faculty. These are broad specifications indeed. It has been suggested that this very broadness has disturbed college administrators, who suggest that at some point a college should say its book stock is large enough to permit adding of new titles at the expense of some that are no longer sufficiently useful to justify the space they occupy. Librarians acknowledge that an optimum size of library sounds entirely reasonable, but they then turn to a description of collections that suggests that arriving at an optimum size of a book collection may be almost as difficult, and very similar to, arriving at a statement as to the optimum amount of money a friend should be allowed to accumulate. I suggest that there must be answers to some of these questions, and we should set about trying to find them. Before we turn away from book collections, we should recognize that the librarian's tendency to accept gifts of doubtful utility, to create special collections of one kind or another, and to assume other obligations that may divert staff and space from more direct, curricular needs have not gone unnoticed and may be open to more critical questioning in the future than they have in the past.

In staffing, government, and control, the conference reveals the greatest amount of uncertainty. The library is under an extraordinary variety of pressures, some of them clearly in direct conflict with one another. The pressures are likely to create demands well in excess of the resources, and many kinds of decisions must be made that tend to involve highly subjective judgments. For these reasons the limitations faced by the library are likely not to be known or well understood by either the faculty or the college administration; yet the objectives and policies of the library must be kept in harmony with those of the college. The librarian appears to be isolated from the president by his very uniqueness, and he is often isolated from those groups or committees in which faculty policies are formulated or decisions are made. Such isolation presents serious difficulties for the able and conscientious librarian. The library committee at its best cannot fully overcome such isolation, though the good committee can be of tremendous assistance to the librarian. At its worst, the committee can try to operate the library and make decisions that the librarian ought to make. It may well be that the fear that the library committee will try to interfere in the administrative responsibilities of the competent librarian and that it must therefore be kept purely advisory has been exaggerated, to the detriment of an effective and mutually responsible working relationship. A committee which had certain broad policy and legislative powers vested in it might be a constructive force in the college. Its discussions might then even be directed toward issues of more basic importance than those suggested by the author-experts. Certainly there seems to be much room for research, investigation, and study that will give us a better understanding of those factors that produce healthy and harmonious relationships between the college administration, the faculty, and the library.

What kind of people succeed best in college-library work and what kind of training they need may be difficult questions to answer until we are prepared to be more specific than we can be today about the true functions of the college library. For surely it is the functions of the library that will determine the nature and the quality of the library service. Are librarians teachers, are they subject-literature specialists, or are they something else? There even appears to be a conflict in the views of the conference speakers as to whether the college librarians have the primary function of book selection, with the advice of the faculty when needed, or whether the faculty must carry the major burden of selection. If so basic a responsibility is still in doubt, how can we decide what kind of personnel is needed and the kind of training the personnel must have?

There is evidence that we may be failing to communicate well with both faculty members and college administrators, and I raise the question of whether, when we do communicate, we are talking about the right things. The library, though humanistic in many of its patterns of use, is a social institution that can be studied, and it can be improved as our understanding of the library grows. But the library does not exist in a vacuum, and it does not exist to serve itself. We must be sure that our presidents and our faculties have as clear a picture of the library as we can give them. In doing this we must avoid trying to measure things that are not measurable, and we must not measure things that are not worth measuring. We must be prepared to make the same kind of value judgments that a faculty is constantly forced to make. We must continue to develop a sound body of principles and knowledge that both we and our academic colleagues will understand and be able to follow with confidence. This will not make librarianship any simpler—for there will always be frontiers—but it will make libraries better.

A liberal or any other kind of higher education without books—speaking broadly as now we must—is an apparent contradiction. Despite many major problems relating to the college library, the papers and the discussions during this conference also suggest that the good college librarian is likely to be well ahead of many of his faculty and administrative colleagues in his recognition of some of the critical elements that go into the making of good higher education. If, indeed, we are sometimes ahead of our academic colleagues, let us stay there, though not so far that we completely separate ourselves from them; if we are not ahead, then we should, with the full resources of the college library at our command, get there.